JUMBLE® WORKOUT

PUZZLES TO MAKE YOUR HEART RACE!

T0192975

Jeff Knurek
and
David L. Hoyt

TRIUMPH
B O O K S

This book is available in quantity at special discounts
for your group or organization.

For further information, contact:

Triumph Books LLC
814 North Franklin Street
Chicago, Illinois 60610
Phone: (312) 337-0747
www.triumphbooks.com

Printed in U.S.A.

ISBN: 978-1-60078-943-4

Design by Sue Knopf

CONTENTS

JUMBLE®
WORKOUT

CLASSIC
PUZZLES

JUMBLE®

Unscramble these four Jumbles, one letter to
each square, to form four ordinary words.

OTBHO

PUTMH

PSIMRH

OLTETB

SHE THOUGHT HER
SUBWAY RIDE
WAS THIS.

Now arrange the circled letters to form
the surprise answer, as suggested by the
above cartoon.

Print answer here

JUMBLE®

Unscramble these four Jumbles, one letter to each square, to form four ordinary words.

KIPSM

ATUTN

RTOTAH

FMINUF

Eww! I don't think so!

Um...Can I spray you ladies with our latest perfume?

THE SKUNK WOULD PROBABLY GET FIRED FROM HER JOB BECAUSE SHE ---

Now arrange the circled letters to form the surprise answer, as suggested by the above cartoon.

Print answer here

3

JUMBLE®

Unscramble these four Jumbles, one letter to each square, to form four ordinary words.

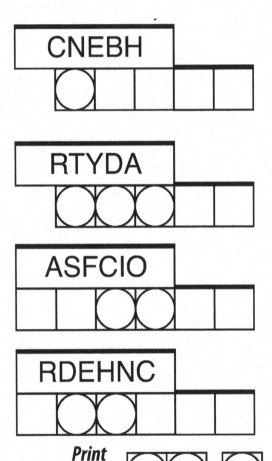

CNEBH

RTYDA

ASFCIO

RDEHNC

He's amazing! One day everyone will know the drummer named Richard Starkey

Unless, of course, he changes his name.

IT DIDN'T TAKE LONG FOR RICHARD STARKEY'S PARENTS TO REALIZE HE WAS GOING TO ----

Now arrange the circled letters to form the surprise answer, as suggested by the above cartoon.

Print answer here ☐☐ ☐ " ☐☐☐☐☐ "

4

JUMBLE®

Unscramble these four Jumbles, one letter to each square, to form four ordinary words.

UENQE

PTOEM

FPTIRO

DNICTU

STARTING CONSTRUCTION WITHOUT THE PROPER PAPERWORK WAS ‒‒‒

Now arrange the circled letters to form the surprise answer, as suggested by the above cartoon.

Print answer here

5

JUMBLE®

Unscramble these four Jumbles, one letter to each square, to form four ordinary words.

AHRBO

USIHS

ACMPDA

RELNLO

Ready...Set...

Go!

PUTTING A 30-SECOND TIME LIMIT ON TODAY'S PUZZLE WOULD CAUSE YOU TO DO THIS.

Now arrange the circled letters to form the surprise answer, as suggested by the above cartoon.

Print answer here

JUMBLE®

Unscramble these four Jumbles, one letter to each square, to form four ordinary words.

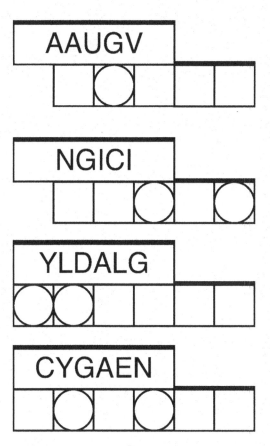

AAUGV

NGICI

YLDALG

CYGAEN

Could you bring the rest down from upstairs?

LOADING THE LUGGAGE FOR THEIR VACATION WAS A CHORE BECAUSE OF ALL THE ---

Now arrange the circled letters to form the surprise answer, as suggested by the above cartoon.

Print answer here

7

JUMBLE®

Unscramble these four Jumbles, one letter to
each square, to form four ordinary words.

LAAHP

RMUYK

LTETEK

AWNEKE

That was way
more expensive
than I expected.

Fil-R-Up
01

DeLa Hoyt
Beachfront Hotel
Just ahead

WITH THE HIGH PRICE OF
GAS, A FULL TANK CAN
LEAD TO ---

Now arrange the circled letters to form
the surprise answer, as suggested by the
above cartoon.

*Print
answer* AN
here

8

JUMBLE®

Unscramble these four Jumbles, one letter to
each square, to form four ordinary words.

LSYIK

HCTIK

AFBELF

DLPUED

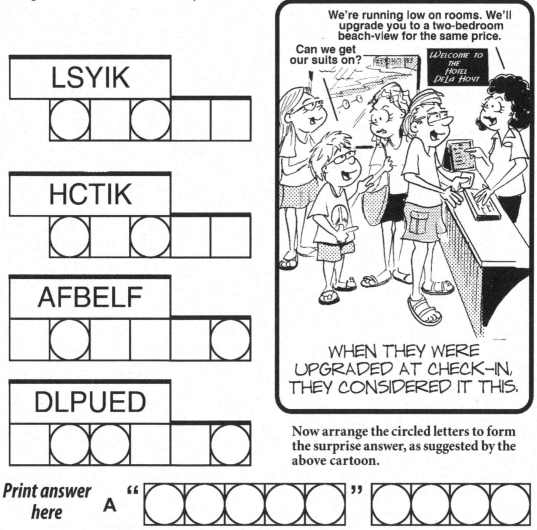

We're running low on rooms. We'll
upgrade you to a two-bedroom
beach-view for the same price.

Can we get
our suits on?

WELCOME TO
THE
HOTEL
DELA HOYT

WHEN THEY WERE
UPGRADED AT CHECK-IN,
THEY CONSIDERED IT THIS.

Now arrange the circled letters to form
the surprise answer, as suggested by the
above cartoon.

Print answer
here

A " ◯◯◯◯◯ " ◯◯◯◯

JUMBLE®

Unscramble these four Jumbles, one letter to each square, to form four ordinary words.

HBMTU

TXSIY

YRTPET

DRURDE

THEIR DAY AT
THE BEACH
DID THIS.

Now arrange the circled letters to form the surprise answer, as suggested by the above cartoon.

Print answer here

JUMBLE®

Unscramble these four Jumbles, one letter to
each square, to form four ordinary words.

NEUDC

OORTB

ACOTRV

UBELOD

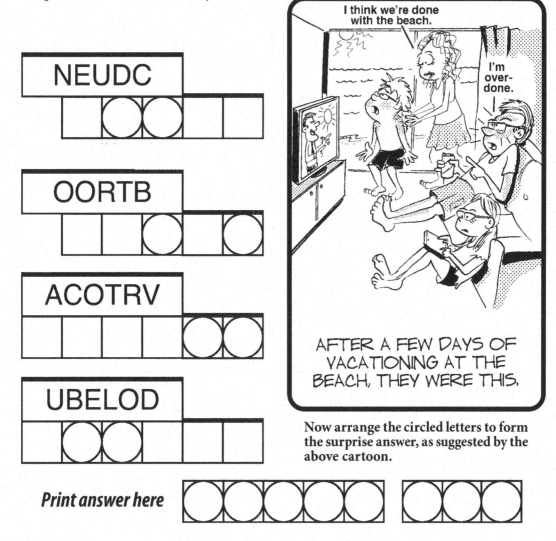

I think we're done
with the beach.

I'm
over-
done.

AFTER A FEW DAYS OF
VACATIONING AT THE
BEACH, THEY WERE THIS.

Now arrange the circled letters to form
the surprise answer, as suggested by the
above cartoon.

Print answer here

11

JUMBLE®

Unscramble these four Jumbles, one letter to
each square, to form four ordinary words.

UEFTL

LOFDO

LAEBTL

HEBAEV

I think it's really
going to appreciate
over time.

This is the perfect spot
to build our home. It's
underpriced.

AVAILABLE

THEY BOUGHT THE
SUBDIVISION PARCEL
BECAUSE THEY THOUGHT
IT HAD THIS.

Now arrange the circled letters to form
the surprise answer, as suggested by the
above cartoon.

Print
answer   A
here

JUMBLE®

Unscramble these four Jumbles, one letter to each square, to form four ordinary words.

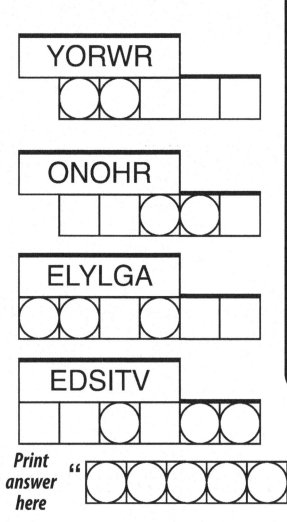

YORWR

ONOHR

ELYLGA

EDSITV

I bet it would be fun to drive on the Autobahn.

Are we taking it on vacation?

HIS NEW ELECTRIC CAR WAS A ----

Now arrange the circled letters to form the surprise answer, as suggested by the above cartoon.

Print answer here

"   "

13

JUMBLE®

Unscramble these four Jumbles, one letter to each square, to form four ordinary words.

CTMHA

LUNEC

OIVNIS

RALIDZ

MicroCola

I think these cans are just the right size for a quick drink.

Oh! They're so cute!

THE MINNEAPOLIS BEVERAGE MAKER HOPED TO HAVE A BIG SUCCESS WITH THIS.

Now arrange the circled letters to form the surprise answer, as suggested by the above cartoon.

Print answer here "◯◯◯◯ ◯◯◯◯"

14

JUMBLE®

Unscramble these four Jumbles, one letter to
each square, to form four ordinary words.

MLIBC

FRDTA

SOGIPS

OIGLEA

THE OLYMPIC
RUNNER LIKED TO
REMEMBER
THE ---

Now arrange the circled letters to form
the surprise answer, as suggested by the
above cartoon.

Print answer here

15

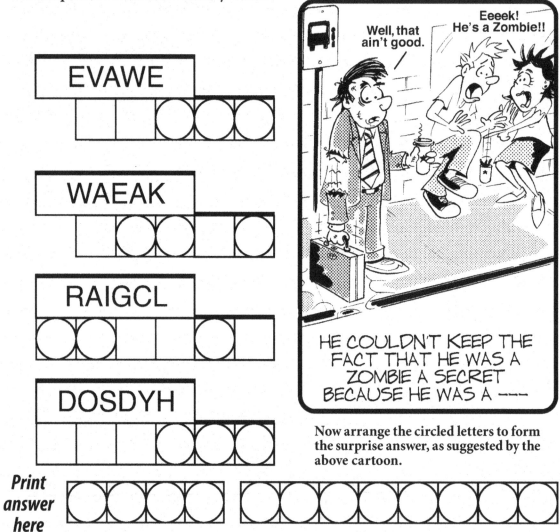

JUMBLE®

Unscramble these four Jumbles, one letter to each square, to form four ordinary words.

EVAWE

WAEAK

RAIGCL

DOSDYH

HE COULDN'T KEEP THE FACT THAT HE WAS A ZOMBIE A SECRET BECAUSE HE WAS A ---

Now arrange the circled letters to form the surprise answer, as suggested by the above cartoon.

Print answer here

JUMBLE®

Unscramble these four Jumbles, one letter to each square, to form four ordinary words.

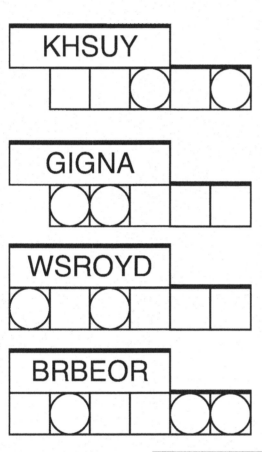

KHSUY

GIGNA

WSROYD

BRBEOR

I think we will prosper in the coming quarters.

IN LOVING MEMORY

·CHARLES·

FOUNDED IN 1898, FRANK SEIBERLING'S TIRE AND RUBBER COMPANY HAS HAD MANY ----

Now arrange the circled letters to form the surprise answer, as suggested by the above cartoon.

Print answer here

17

JUMBLE

Unscramble these four Jumbles, one letter to
each square, to form four ordinary words.

RCDOH

LRDWO

MEOEVR

EBEFEL

Watch it buddy!
I know where you
parked your car!

BEING SHOT AT BY
THE HUNTERS PUT THE
DUCK IN THIS.

Now arrange the circled letters to form
the surprise answer, as suggested by the
above cartoon.

*Print answer
here*   A "◯◯◯◯" ◯◯◯◯

JUMBLE®

Unscramble these four Jumbles, one letter to each square, to form four ordinary words.

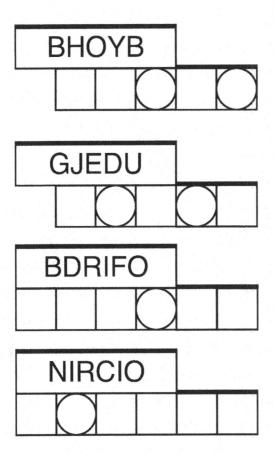

BHOYB

GJEDU

BDRIFO

NIRCIO

How did I get so dirty?

BUG OFF

HOW SHE FELT AFTER SPRAYING THE LAWN FOR INSECTS

Now arrange the circled letters to form the surprise answer, as suggested by the above cartoon.

Print answer here

JUMBLE®

Unscramble these four Jumbles, one letter to
each square, to form four ordinary words.

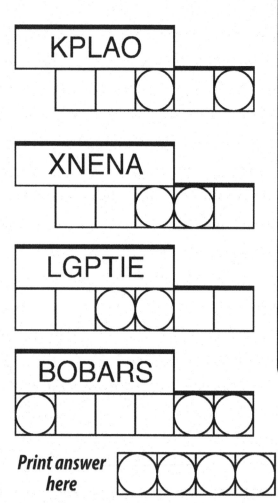

KPLAO

XNENA

LGPTIE

BOBARS

I remember
learning
about that in
school.

It sounded its last clear
note, legend has it,
in honor of George
Washington's birthday
in 1832.

HIS EXPLANATION OF HOW
THE FAMOUS CRACK
FORMED DID THIS.

Now arrange the circled letters to form
the surprise answer, as suggested by the
above cartoon.

*Print answer
here*

JUMBLE®

Unscramble these four Jumbles, one letter to
each square, to form four ordinary words.

FSTIH

WOCNL

EBCDUR

ASNKHE

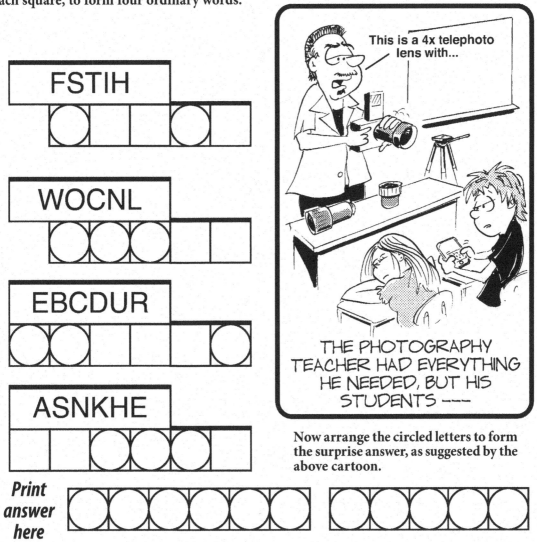

THE PHOTOGRAPHY
TEACHER HAD EVERYTHING
HE NEEDED, BUT HIS
STUDENTS ---

Now arrange the circled letters to form
the surprise answer, as suggested by the
above cartoon.

*Print
answer
here*

JUMBLE®

Unscramble these four Jumbles, one letter to each square, to form four ordinary words.

VAROB

MAGOE

SWORYD

RUCEBH

I love the Manhattan skyline.

Can I ride the donkeys?

WHEN THEY WENT TO NEW YORK CITY, THEY SAW THESE.

Now arrange the circled letters to form the surprise answer, as suggested by the above cartoon.

Print answer here

JUMBLE®

Unscramble these four Jumbles, one letter to each square, to form four ordinary words.

ZOAKO

ORNPE

AALIPM

ATDBAE

I loved reading this. My first husband hated it. He was an idiot. My third husband liked it. He was nice. I can't remember how my second husband felt about it.

THE LIBRARIAN WAS VERY CLEAR ABOUT HOW SHE FELT BECAUSE SHE WAS ----

Now arrange the circled letters to form the surprise answer, as suggested by the above cartoon.

Print answer here AN ◯◯◯◯ ◯◯◯◯

PUZZLE 23

JUMBLE®

Unscramble these four Jumbles, one letter to each square, to form four ordinary words.

RGFOO

DILEY

GIAEMP

NAASTV

We better pick up the pace. I wanted to be on the road before 1 PM.

LONG HAUL RENTALS

IF THEY WANTED TO HAVE EVERYTHING PACKED UP ON TIME, THEY'D NEED TO ---

Now arrange the circled letters to form the surprise answer, as suggested by the above cartoon.

Print answer here

JUMBLE®

Unscramble these four Jumbles, one letter to
each square, to form four ordinary words.

YHERM

DEERL

ALOHMO

GUINGR

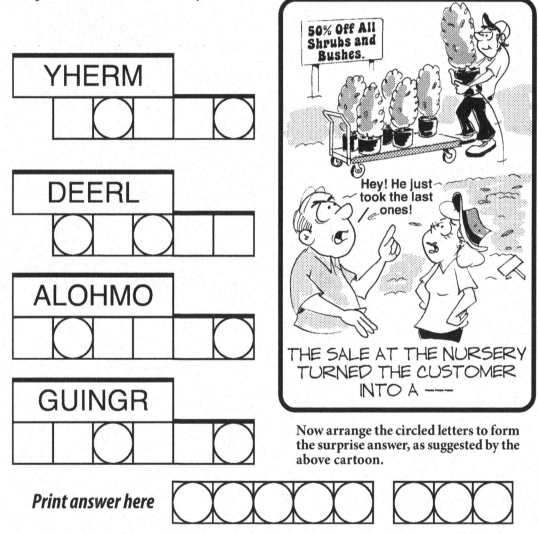

50% Off All
Shrubs and
Bushes.

Hey! He just
took the last
ones!

THE SALE AT THE NURSERY
TURNED THE CUSTOMER
INTO A ---

Now arrange the circled letters to form
the surprise answer, as suggested by the
above cartoon.

Print answer here

JUMBLE

Unscramble these four Jumbles, one letter to each square, to form four ordinary words.

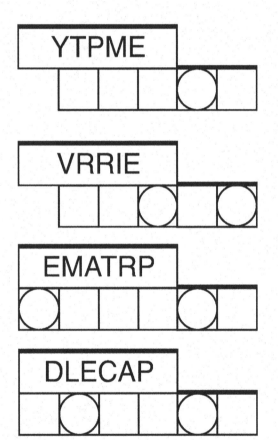

YTPME

VRRIE

EMATRP

DLECAP

Using the gravity of the sun was genius.

REGARDLESS OF WHERE THEY TRAVELED, THIS WAS ALWAYS THE CENTER OF GRAVITY.

Now arrange the circled letters to form the surprise answer, as suggested by the above cartoon.

Print answer here THE

26

JUMBLE®

WORKOUT

DAILY
PUZZLES

JUMBLE®

Unscramble these four Jumbles, one letter to each square, to form four ordinary words.

DNTAS

MGOUB

TIHWCT

TOGUIN

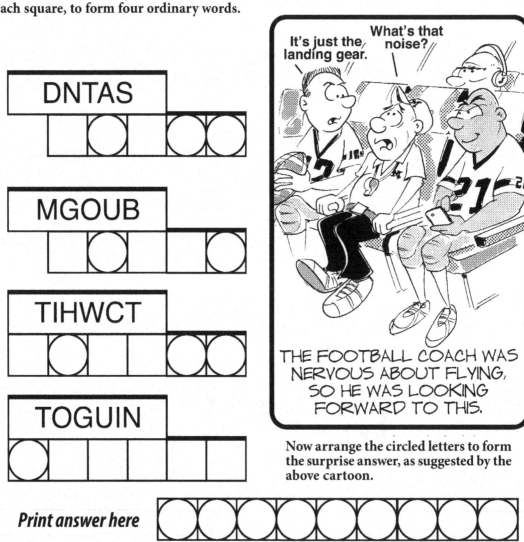

It's just the landing gear.

What's that noise?

THE FOOTBALL COACH WAS NERVOUS ABOUT FLYING, SO HE WAS LOOKING FORWARD TO THIS.

Now arrange the circled letters to form the surprise answer, as suggested by the above cartoon.

Print answer here

JUMBLE®

Unscramble these four Jumbles, one letter to
each square, to form four ordinary words.

CIPYK

OAVLC

TEYLNG

KRONBE

This doesn't
surprise
me at all.

Same results
as our last
100 attempts.

WHEN THEIR NUCLEAR
FUSION EXPERIMENT
FAILED AGAIN, THE
SCIENTISTS HAD ----

Now arrange the circled letters to form
the surprise answer, as suggested by the
above cartoon.

*Print
answer
here*

JUMBLE®

Unscramble these four Jumbles, one letter to each square, to form four ordinary words.

FTRNO

GBYGA

NOIWNM

DEDPDA

$1,000 STORE
EVERYTHING $1000

WELCOME SHOPPERS!

Don't they mean Dollar Store?

This is ridiculous! It will never work. I will never go in that store.

EVEN WITH ONE, THE THOUSAND-DOLLAR STORE WAS NOT GOING TO BE A SUCCESS.

Now arrange the circled letters to form the surprise answer, as suggested by the above cartoon.

Print answer here

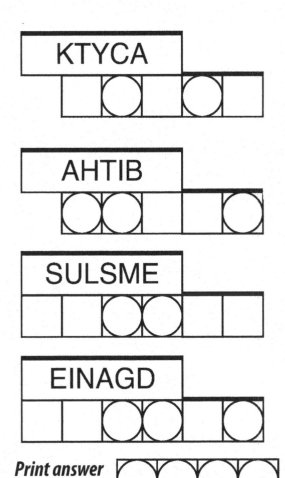

JUMBLE.

Unscramble these four Jumbles, one letter to each square, to form four ordinary words.

KTYCA

AHTIB

SULSME

EINAGD

Wow! And to think we were just going to have turkey for dinner.

WHEN THE PILGRIMS WERE PRESENTED WITH A FEAST, THEY DID THIS.

Now arrange the circled letters to form the surprise answer, as suggested by the above cartoon.

Print answer here

31

JUMBLE®

Unscramble these four Jumbles, one letter to
each square, to form four ordinary words.

CUORC

EVOCT

CNKOUL

RDSANT

You go
head.
I'll go next.

Thanks!

WHEN THERE WEREN'T
ENOUGH GO-CARTS TO
GO AROUND,
THEY DID THIS.

Now arrange the circled letters to form
the surprise answer, as suggested by the
above cartoon.

Print answer here

JUMBLE®

Unscramble these four Jumbles, one letter to
each square, to form four ordinary words.

TNOEF

LGSIL

EIOCTX

ULEEDG

WHEN THE MEN
ENTERED THE ROOM FOR
THE SPEED DATING, THEY
WENT IN ---

Now arrange the circled letters to form
the surprise answer, as suggested by the
above cartoon.

Print answer here

JUMBLE®

Unscramble these four Jumbles, one letter to
each square, to form four ordinary words.

PTEMY

CLUGH

CIKOEO

SYPRAT

He broke his leg
last year.

It's my fault!
I told him to
"break a leg."

We need to
get you to
the hospital.

To be,
or not
to be,..

WHEN THE ACTOR BROKE
HIS LEG ON-STAGE, THEY
HAD TO ---

Now arrange the circled letters to form
the surprise answer, as suggested by the
above cartoon.

Print answer here

JUMBLE®

Unscramble these four Jumbles, one letter to
each square, to form four ordinary words.

BOMOL

CATHW

FUSYTF

DMAYID

Six more
weeks of
winter for
sure. Now, let
me go back
to sleep.

It's official,
Punxsutawney Phil
declares winter is
sticking around.

PHIL

THE GROUNDHOG
MADE HIS PREDICTION
WITHOUT A ---

Now arrange the circled letters to form
the surprise answer, as suggested by the
above cartoon.

*Print
answer
here*

OF
A

JUMBLE®

Unscramble these four Jumbles, one letter to each square, to form four ordinary words.

GRADU

LIGYN

VURSYE

TNEADT

Where are all the customers? Isn't anybody thirsty? I knew I should have gone to medical school!

LEMONADE 5¢

THE LEMONADE IS IN

WHEN NO ONE SHOWED UP TO BUY HER LEMONADE, SHE COULDN'T ---

Now arrange the circled letters to form the surprise answer, as suggested by the above cartoon.

Print answer here

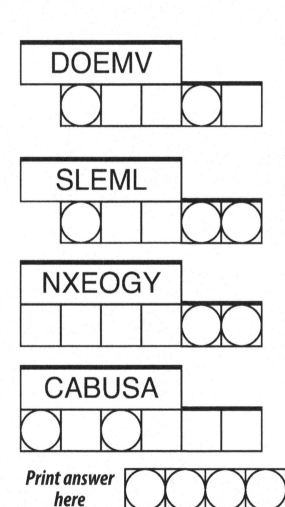

JUMBLE®

Unscramble these four Jumbles, one letter to
each square, to form four ordinary words.

DOEMV

SLEML

NXEOGY

CABUSA

This looks familiar.

How many shoe stores can you have?

ONCE YOU'VE LOOKED AT
ONE SHOPPING CENTER,
YOU'VE ----

Now arrange the circled letters to form
the surprise answer, as suggested by the
above cartoon.

Print answer here

JUMBLE®

Unscramble these four Jumbles, one letter to each square, to form four ordinary words.

YDUBD

MARCP

TUNBOY

SMYORT

WHEN SHE ASKED IF SHE WOULD BE ABLE TO GET A SEAT ON THE NEXT FLIGHT, SHE WAS TOLD TO ---

Now arrange the circled letters to form the surprise answer, as suggested by the above cartoon.

Print answer here

38

JUMBLE®

Unscramble these four Jumbles, one letter to
each square, to form four ordinary words.

AZLEB

ACHHT

BETJOC

SLOIAR

That's our
son.

You must be
very proud.

PLAYING THE SUN IN THE
PLAY ABOUT THE SOLAR
SYSTEM ALLOWED
HIM TO ---

Now arrange the circled letters to form
the surprise answer, as suggested by the
above cartoon.

Print answer here

JUMBLE®

Unscramble these four Jumbles, one letter to
each square, to form four ordinary words.

TRNIP

LWAOL

SALSCY

TRREEV

I like to hear
every sound
from every
direction.

This is
different.

HIS UNIQUE
SOUND SYSTEM
WASN'T THIS.

Now arrange the circled letters to form
the surprise answer, as suggested by the
above cartoon.

*Print
answer
here*

JUMBLE®

Unscramble these four Jumbles, one letter to each square, to form four ordinary words.

LEYCC

NOWDU

ABEENT

TARENB

You're doing great, honey!

This place is dead.

I thought we'd have a bigger turnout.

THE CONCERT IN DEATH VALLEY HAD ----

Now arrange the circled letters to form the surprise answer, as suggested by the above cartoon.

Print answer here

41

JUMBLE®

Unscramble these four Jumbles, one letter to
each square, to form four ordinary words.

RAWEF

ZEOON

LATERL

CADFAE

WHEN THE MARATHON
RUNNER MISSED THE RIGHT
TURN, HE ENDED UP ----

Now arrange the circled letters to form
the surprise answer, as suggested by the
above cartoon.

**Print answer
here**

42

JUMBLE®

Unscramble these four Jumbles, one letter to each square, to form four ordinary words.

EUCIJ

KLANP

SEYPLE

ZFLEIZ

Oh, no! I worked for days on this!

WHEN HER JIGSAW PUZZLE WAS RUINED, SHE DID THIS.

Now arrange the circled letters to form the surprise answer, as suggested by the above cartoon.

Print answer here

TO

JUMBLE®

Unscramble these four Jumbles, one letter to
each square, to form four ordinary words.

ASYET

BLAFE

TOBREH

BLEMME

Here's a little more
made with love.

I love
you!

HIS VALENTINE'S DAY
LUNCH WAS THIS.

Now arrange the circled letters to form
the surprise answer, as suggested by the
above cartoon.

*Print
answer
here* A

44

JUMBLE®

Unscramble these four Jumbles, one letter to each square, to form four ordinary words.

CYYUK

EZIRP

ANRUFI

TCEALT

What a waste of time.

Those guys are insane. Men weren't meant to fly. It will never get off the ground.

SOME PEOPLE THOUGHT THE WRIGHT BROTHERS WERE JUST ---

Now arrange the circled letters to form the surprise answer, as suggested by the above cartoon.

Print answer here

" ◯◯◯◯◯ " ◯◯◯◯◯

45

JUMBLE®

Unscramble these four Jumbles, one letter to
each square, to form four ordinary words.

TAHIF

FRASC

RECCAS

FLAWEF

I don't have the
money for a new
car.

You can
have my
bus pass.

CARELESS DRIVERS
CAN END UP ----

Now arrange the circled letters to form
the surprise answer, as suggested by the
above cartoon.

Print answer here " ◯◯◯ - ◯◯◯◯ "

46

JUMBLE®

Unscramble these four Jumbles, one letter to each square, to form four ordinary words.

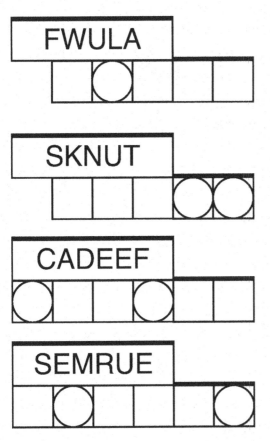

FWULA

SKNUT

CADEEF

SEMRUE

I can barely type.

You need to stay in bed the next two days.

GETTING THE FLU ON A FRIDAY MAKES FOR THIS.

Now arrange the circled letters to form the surprise answer, as suggested by the above cartoon.

Print answer here A " ◯◯◯◯ - ◯◯◯ "

JUMBLE®

Unscramble these four Jumbles, one letter to each square, to form four ordinary words.

RLIGL

EVNOM

CLINHF

BARTEY

Did you know that it's a leap year?

Great! I'll spend my bonus day reading.

IN A LEAP YEAR, WHICH MONTHS HAVE 29 DAYS?

Now arrange the circled letters to form the surprise answer, as suggested by the above cartoon.

Print answer here

JUMBLE®

Unscramble these four Jumbles, one letter to
each square, to form four ordinary words.

GAOCN

VRAAL

NRHUCC

SIBEED

If you keep studying,
you'll get the hang of this.

This parabola stuff is new to me.

SHE WAS STRUGGLING IN
GEOMETRY CLASS BECAUSE
THERE WAS A ---

Now arrange the circled letters to form
the surprise answer, as suggested by the
above cartoon.

Print answer here

JUMBLE

Unscramble these four Jumbles, one letter to each square, to form four ordinary words.

FDTAR

HUORG

SMADEK

TECPIO

Let's go to the Welcome Center to get a map, then go explore.

Old Faithful 4 m
Welcome
Center   1 m
P 1 mile on left

Welcome to YELLOWSTONE NATIONAL

BEFORE THEIR ADVENTURES AT YELLOWSTONE COULD BEGIN, THEY NEEDED TO DO THIS.

Now arrange the circled letters to form the surprise answer, as suggested by the above cartoon.

Print answer here

50

JUMBLE®

Unscramble these four Jumbles, one letter to
each square, to form four ordinary words.

PRUEP

GINIC

GOTROF

TARYAS

Will it be
ready for this
Sunday?

Trust me. It's
the only thing
we're working
on.

PUTTING THE SPIRE
ON THE BUILDING
WAS THIS.

Now arrange the circled letters to form
the surprise answer, as suggested by the
above cartoon.

Print
answer
here

JUMBLE®

Unscramble these four Jumbles, one letter to
each square, to form four ordinary words.

ENKTL

NSURP

CUTALA

CRENTH

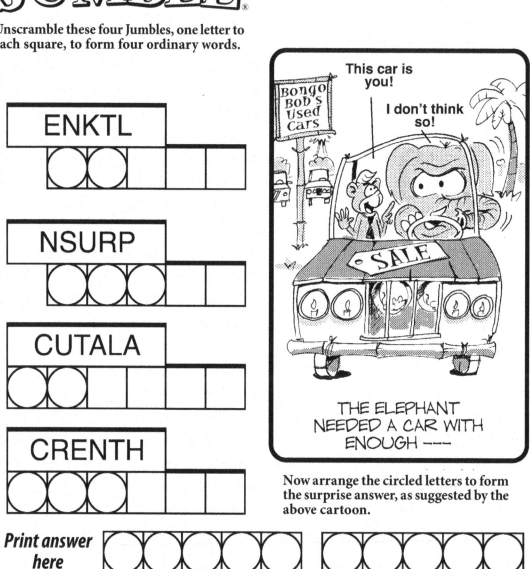

Bongo
Bob's
Used
Cars

This car is
you!

I don't think
so!

SALE

THE ELEPHANT
NEEDED A CAR WITH
ENOUGH ---

Now arrange the circled letters to form
the surprise answer, as suggested by the
above cartoon.

*Print answer
here*

JUMBLE®

Unscramble these four Jumbles, one letter to each square, to form four ordinary words.

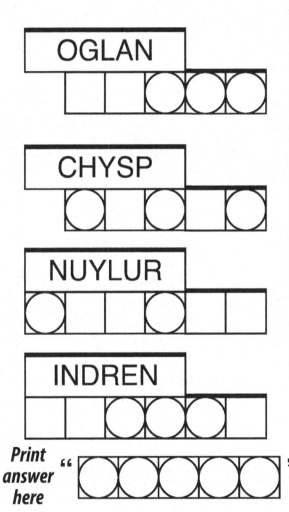

OGLAN

CHYSP

NUYLUR

INDREN

...and then the guy finds a rowboat in a row of corn...

I'm not drawing that. You can do better. Try again.

HE REFUSED TO DRAW THE JUMBLE CARTOON BECAUSE THE IDEA BEHIND IT WASN'T THIS.

Now arrange the circled letters to form the surprise answer, as suggested by the above cartoon.

Print answer here " ◯◯◯◯◯ " ◯◯◯◯◯◯

JUMBLE®

Unscramble these four Jumbles, one letter to
each square, to form four ordinary words.

KNIBL

MAIDT

FSIXUF

CREGRO

I'll be right back
with the rest.

Thank you!
Thank you
very much.

ELVIS LIKED TO
EAT MEALS THAT
WERE THIS.

Now arrange the circled letters to form
the surprise answer, as suggested by the
above cartoon.

Print
answer
here

JUMBLE®

Unscramble these four Jumbles, one letter to
each square, to form four ordinary words.

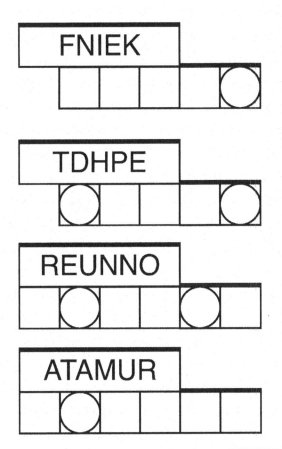

FNIEK

TDHPE

REUNNO

ATAMUR

WHEN THE UNPREPARED
HUNTER RAN INTO THE
GIANT BUCK, HE SAID THIS.

Now arrange the circled letters to form
the surprise answer, as suggested by the
above cartoon.

Print answer here "  "

JUMBLE®

Unscramble these four Jumbles, one letter to each square, to form four ordinary words.

WRABN

CAFET

FUTOIT

TRONDE

I was selling so many cars that I needed to build a new factory.

RIVER ROUGE PLANT

AFTER THE SUCCESS OF HIS MODEL T, HENRY FORD EXPANDED HIS BUSINESS BECAUSE HE COULD ---

Now arrange the circled letters to form the surprise answer, as suggested by the above cartoon.

Print answer here

JUMBLE®

Unscramble these four Jumbles, one letter to each square, to form four ordinary words.

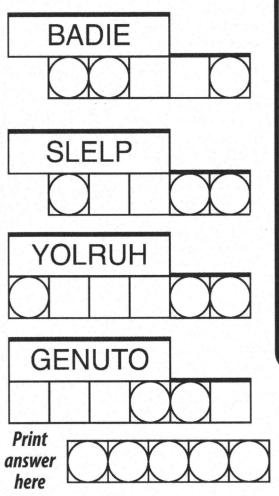

BADIE

SLELP

YOLRUH

GENUTO

BREATH!

The most common craving is for men to be the ones to be pregnant.

WHEN THE BIRTHING CLASS INSTRUCTOR TOLD A JOKE, SHE GOT THIS.

Now arrange the circled letters to form the surprise answer, as suggested by the above cartoon.

Print answer here

JUMBLE®

Unscramble these four Jumbles, one letter to each square, to form four ordinary words.

DEEGH

IDOVA

TREELT

DROIHR

I'll step on it.

My husband will meet us there.

TAXI

WHEN SHE NEEDED TO GET TO THE HOSPITAL IN A HURRY, SHE CALLED A CAB TO ---

Now arrange the circled letters to form the surprise answer, as suggested by the above cartoon.

Print answer here

⬡⬡⬡⬡⬡⬡⬡ ⬡⬡⬡

58

JUMBLE®

Unscramble these four Jumbles, one letter to
each square, to form four ordinary words.

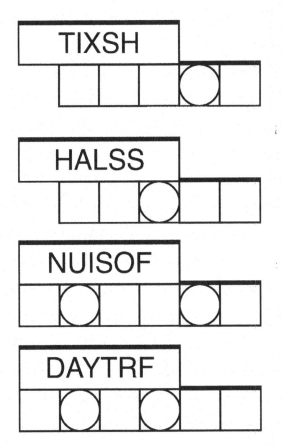

TIXSH

HALSS

NUISOF

DAYTRF

We've discovered
a ninth planet
beyond the orbit
of Neptune.

That's
amazing.

WHEN THEY ANNOUNCED
THE DISCOVERY OF PLUTO
ON 3-13-1930, PEOPLE
THOUGHT IT WAS THIS.

Now arrange the circled letters to form
the surprise answer, as suggested by the
above cartoon.

Print answer here ☐◯◯◯ ◯◯◯◯ !

JUMBLE®

Unscramble these four Jumbles, one letter to each square, to form four ordinary words.

MEOPT

SUGET

CHEELK

TNELAG

They don't stand a chance with this guy making so many shots.

HE DID THIS TO THE OTHER TEAM WHEN HE MADE SO MANY BASKETS.

Now arrange the circled letters to form the surprise answer, as suggested by the above cartoon.

Print answer here ◯◯◯◯ ◯◯◯◯

JUMBLE

Unscramble these four Jumbles, one letter to
each square, to form four ordinary words.

ESVOH

YDOLD

SWUNIE

UNDARO

They're going
to be here any
second. They
look angry!

Is this a
joke?

THE ZOMBIE WAS THIS
WHEN HE WARNED THAT
HUMANS WERE
APPROACHING.

Now arrange the circled letters to form
the surprise answer, as suggested by the
above cartoon.

Print
answer
here

61

JUMBLE®

Unscramble these four Jumbles, one letter to each square, to form four ordinary words.

FTOAO

AGLUH

DIRALA

FODFAR

It uses 75% less coal!

No way can it be that much more efficient.

Liar!

WHEN JAMES WATT TALKED ABOUT HIS STEAM ENGINE, SOME PEOPLE THOUGHT HE WAS ---

Now arrange the circled letters to form the surprise answer, as suggested by the above cartoon.

Print answer here

JUMBLE®

Unscramble these four Jumbles, one letter to each square, to form four ordinary words.

THCUH

DEAAG

ENOCAB

WRROOS

It really relaxes and inspires me.

What are you doing in there?

AFTER A LONG DAY OF MAKING CARTOONS, THE JUMBLE ARTIST DID THIS.

Now arrange the circled letters to form the surprise answer, as suggested by the above cartoon.

Print answer here

63

JUMBLE®

Unscramble these four Jumbles, one letter to each square, to form four ordinary words.

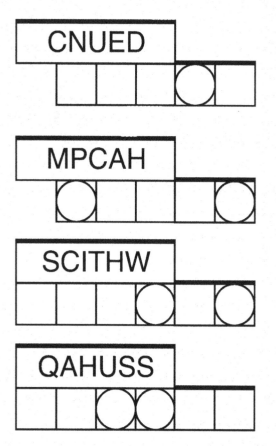

CNUED

MPCAH

SCITHW

QAHUSS

Hurry! The game has already started.

HE WAS RUNNING BEHIND WITH HIS MUSTARD DELIVERIES AND NEEDED TO DO THIS.

Now arrange the circled letters to form the surprise answer, as suggested by the above cartoon.

Print answer here

JUMBLE®

Unscramble these four Jumbles, one letter to each square, to form four ordinary words.

NPUED

ACYED

KOIROE

TEFDIT

Hey! This isn't the top that we saw in the store.

Were they trying to fool us?

WHEN HE INSTALLED HIS NEW KITCHEN, HE REALIZED THAT HIS GRANITE WAS THIS.

Now arrange the circled letters to form the surprise answer, as suggested by the above cartoon.

Print answer here

JUMBLE®

Unscramble these four Jumbles, one letter to each square, to form four ordinary words.

DOFOL

SWNOH

NNGIEE

SCUACE

I've been looking forward to this day.

BREAKING NHL RECORDS WAS THIS TO WAYNE GRETZKY.

Now arrange the circled letters to form the surprise answer, as suggested by the above cartoon.

Print answer here

⬡⬡⬡ OF ⬡⬡⬡ ⬡⬡⬡⬡⬡

JUMBLE®

Unscramble these four Jumbles, one letter to each square, to form four ordinary words.

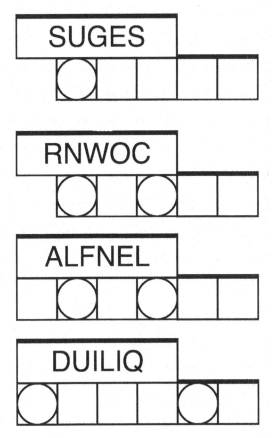

SUGES

RNWOC

ALFNEL

DUILIQ

No arguing with that.

Great face! And that hand gesture he uses is catchy. He's perfect.

STAR TREK

THEIR CHOICE OF LEONARD NIMOY TO PLAY SPOCK WAS THIS.

Now arrange the circled letters to form the surprise answer, as suggested by the above cartoon.

Print answer here

JUMBLE®

Unscramble these four Jumbles, one letter to each square, to form four ordinary words.

AVEEW

KNRUD

NOONIT

DIALNS

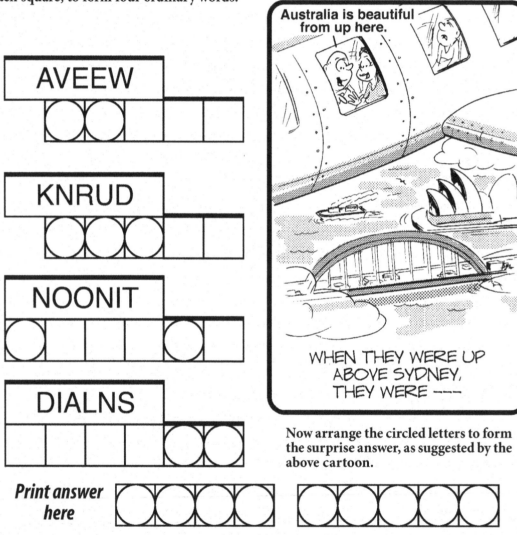

Australia is beautiful from up here.

WHEN THEY WERE UP ABOVE SYDNEY, THEY WERE ----

Now arrange the circled letters to form the surprise answer, as suggested by the above cartoon.

Print answer here

JUMBLE®

Unscramble these four Jumbles, one letter to
each square, to form four ordinary words.

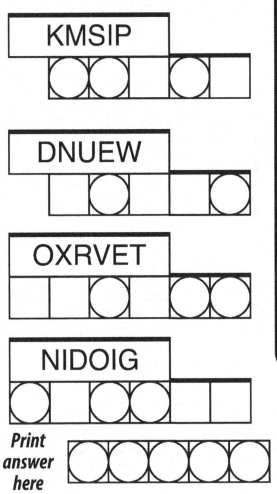

KMSIP

DNUEW

OXRVET

NIDOIG

This isn't what I ordered.

WHEN THE WAITRESS
GAVE THEM THE
WRONG COCKTAILS,
THEY HAD ---

Now arrange the circled letters to form
the surprise answer, as suggested by the
above cartoon.

**Print
answer
here**

JUMBLE®

Unscramble these four Jumbles, one letter to
each square, to form four ordinary words.

WERAA

HILWE

TEYUBA

TRAGEH

This script is
awesome!

HELEN HUNT
WAS ANXIOUS TO STAR IN
"TWISTER" AFTER THE
SCRIPT ---

Now arrange the circled letters to form
the surprise answer, as suggested by the
above cartoon.

Print
answer
here

70

JUMBLE®

Unscramble these four Jumbles, one letter to each square, to form four ordinary words.

INVEX

GIDUL

SCAWTH

BEAZAL

How can I pick up riders in this?

THE STORM DAMAGED THE TAXI WHEN IT DID THIS.

Now arrange the circled letters to form the surprise answer, as suggested by the above cartoon.

Print answer here

JUMBLE®

Unscramble these four Jumbles, one letter to
each square, to form four ordinary words.

YAMLD

FIUNY

ANUDIP

BEELBP

Hi, folks! You look like you need
a car today! What's it going to
take to have you driving away
with my newest model?

HOW THE PUSHY
SALESMAN
SAID HELLO.

Now arrange the circled letters to form
the surprise answer, as suggested by the
above cartoon.

Print answer here " ◯◯◯ - ◯◯◯ "

JUMBLE®

Unscramble these four Jumbles, one letter to each square, to form four ordinary words.

UISES

GILCO

JIRUNY

FCAETF

I have this sketch of what I am envisioning. I'm a little bit of a fashion trendsetter.

Oookay?!

WHEN HE ASKED FOR A CUSTOM-MADE TUXEDO, THE TAILOR SAID THIS----

Now arrange the circled letters to form the surprise answer, as suggested by the above cartoon.

Print answer here

73

JUMBLE®

Unscramble these four Jumbles, one letter to each square, to form four ordinary words.

DNELB

PLIEM

TAISCT

ALIYES

PEOPLE FROM BANGOR
WHO GET CARRIED AWAY
WITH THEIR STATE
PRIDE ARE ---

Now arrange the circled letters to form the surprise answer, as suggested by the above cartoon.

Print answer here " ◯◯◯◯◯◯ - ◯◯◯◯ "

JUMBLE®

Unscramble these four Jumbles, one letter to
each square, to form four ordinary words.

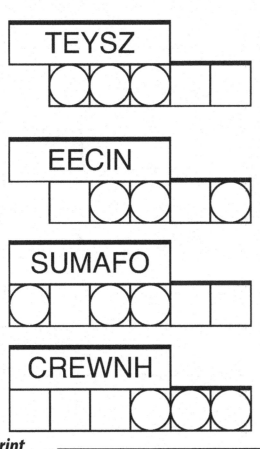

TEYSZ

EECIN

SUMAFO

CREWNH

Aaaayy! What are you
doing? I'm the real
Henry Winkler!
Meet ....
As Seen On
"Happy Days"!

Jumb
Here

HIS ATTEMPT
TO IMPERSONATE
HENRY WINKLER WAS A ---

Now arrange the circled letters to form
the surprise answer, as suggested by the
above cartoon.

*Print
answer
here*

"  "

JUMBLE®

Unscramble these four Jumbles, one letter to
each square, to form four ordinary words.

SMTUY

YXTIS

BNELBI

CAFORT

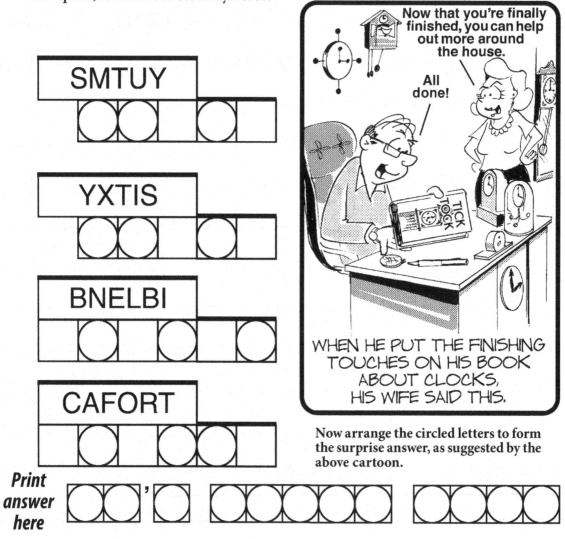

Now that you're finally
finished, you can help
out more around
the house.

All
done!

TICK
TOCK

WHEN HE PUT THE FINISHING
TOUCHES ON HIS BOOK
ABOUT CLOCKS,
HIS WIFE SAID THIS.

Now arrange the circled letters to form
the surprise answer, as suggested by the
above cartoon.

Print
answer
here

⬜⬜'⬜   ⬜⬜⬜⬜⬜   ⬜⬜⬜⬜

JUMBLE®

Unscramble these four Jumbles, one letter to each square, to form four ordinary words.

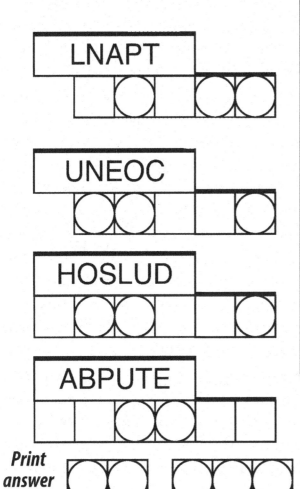

LNAPT

UNEOC

HOSLUD

ABPUTE

Come on! Quickly. I need the answers now!

2 X 2
420 X 2
650 X 2
217 X 2

HOW THE MATH TEACHER EXPECTED HER STUDENTS TO RESPOND.

Now arrange the circled letters to form the surprise answer, as suggested by the above cartoon.

Print answer here

77

JUMBLE®

Unscramble these four Jumbles, one letter to
each square, to form four ordinary words.

TRNUG

LEERD

SKNIRH

PEIEAC

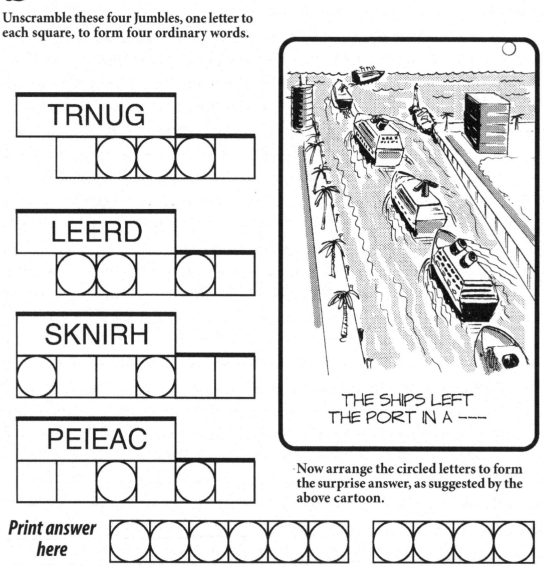

THE SHIPS LEFT
THE PORT IN A ----

Now arrange the circled letters to form
the surprise answer, as suggested by the
above cartoon.

**Print answer
here**

JUMBLE®

Unscramble these four Jumbles, one letter to
each square, to form four ordinary words.

USPOY

GITFH

TACIVY

TCLIHG

Can you help me?
I think I broke
my wrist.

Can't you see
we're busy?

Go stand
over there!

AFTER GETTING TO THE
EMERGENCY ROOM, HE WAS
HOPING FOR SOME ----

Now arrange the circled letters to form
the surprise answer, as suggested by the
above cartoon.

**Print answer
here**

JUMBLE®

Unscramble these four Jumbles, one letter to each square, to form four ordinary words.

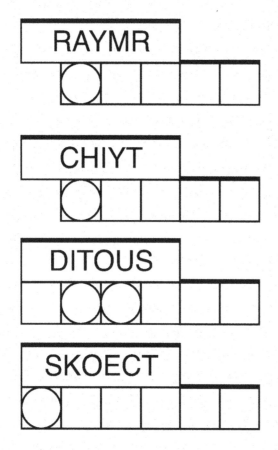

RAYMR

CHIYT

DITOUS

SKOECT

A 200-foot rope plus two 100-foot ropes should be enough.

Are you sure that's going to be enough to reach the top?

WHEN ADDING UP HOW MUCH ROPE HE'D NEED FOR THE CLIMB, HE WOULD DO THIS.

Now arrange the circled letters to form the surprise answer, as suggested by the above cartoon.

Print answer here

JUMBLE®

Unscramble these four Jumbles, one letter to each square, to form four ordinary words.

SCURH

HICTK

TUDNOL

MOYMER

Oh, say can you see...

REGARDLESS OF THE STYLE IT'S PERFORMED IN, A NATIONAL ANTHEM IS THIS.

Now arrange the circled letters to form the surprise answer, as suggested by the above cartoon.

Print answer here

JUMBLE®

Unscramble these four Jumbles, one letter to
each square, to form four ordinary words.

ANFIT

MKSIP

QAOUEP

AHMMEY

Are you crazy!
That ball was
clearly out! You
need glasses!

JOHN MCENROE WOULD
SOMETIMES LOSE HIS
TEMPER TRYING TO ---

Now arrange the circled letters to form
the surprise answer, as suggested by the
above cartoon.

Print
answer
here

JUMBLE®

Unscramble these four Jumbles, one letter to
each square, to form four ordinary words.

VAOCH

CLEEX

DAFIRT

KOEPCT

SIXPENCE PIE-EATING CONTEST

I knew I'd win.
It was easy.
What's for
dessert?

WINNING THE PIE-EATING
CONTEST WAS THIS
FOR HIM.

Now arrange the circled letters to form
the surprise answer, as suggested by the
above cartoon.

*Print
answer* A
here

JUMBLE®

Unscramble these four Jumbles, one letter to
each square, to form four ordinary words.

NIYWD

ARVOF

DISARU

GEIGLG

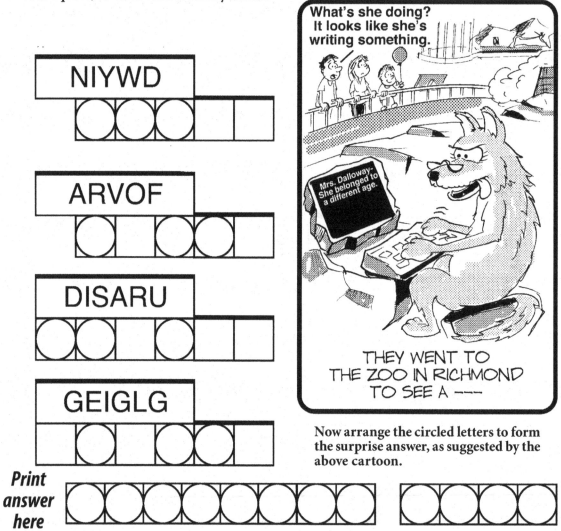

What's she doing?
It looks like she's
writing something.

Mrs. Dalloway.
She belonged to
a different age.

THEY WENT TO
THE ZOO IN RICHMOND
TO SEE A ---

Now arrange the circled letters to form
the surprise answer, as suggested by the
above cartoon.

Print
answer
here

JUMBLE®

Unscramble these four Jumbles, one letter to each square, to form four ordinary words.

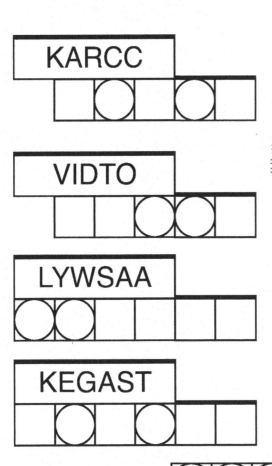

KARCC

VIDTO

LYWSAA

KEGAST

I said, "Hey, you, get off of my cloud!"...

THE CONCERT BY THE VOLCANO FEATURED THIS.

Now arrange the circled letters to form the surprise answer, as suggested by the above cartoon.

Print answer here

85

JUMBLE®

Unscramble these four Jumbles, one letter to each square, to form four ordinary words.

DEEUX

TCEHI

OCADIZ

CEKUTB

So what brings you to Prague?

I just wanted to see what it was like.

HE WENT TO PRAGUE BECAUSE HE WANTED TO DO THIS.

Now arrange the circled letters to form the surprise answer, as suggested by the above cartoon.

Print answer here "◯◯◯◯◯" ◯◯ ◯◯◯

JUMBLE®

Unscramble these four Jumbles, one letter to each square, to form four ordinary words.

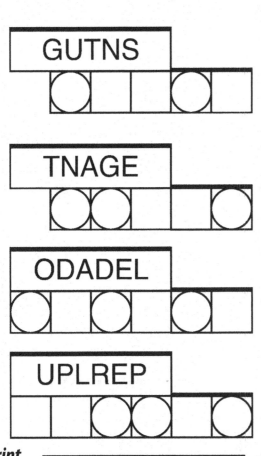

GUTNS

TNAGE

ODADEL

UPLREP

Wow! They're amazing!

THEY WENT TO THE AIR SHOW IN NEBRASKA TO SEE THE ---

Now arrange the circled letters to form the surprise answer, as suggested by the above cartoon.

Print answer here

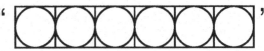

" "

JUMBLE®

Unscramble these four Jumbles, one letter to
each square, to form four ordinary words.

KCARN

UONIN

YORPOD

BEDORT

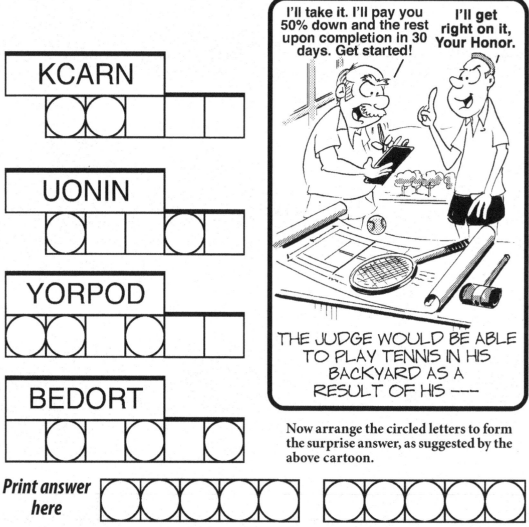

I'll take it. I'll pay you
50% down and the rest
upon completion in 30
days. Get started!

I'll get
right on it,
Your Honor.

THE JUDGE WOULD BE ABLE
TO PLAY TENNIS IN HIS
BACKYARD AS A
RESULT OF HIS ---

Now arrange the circled letters to form
the surprise answer, as suggested by the
above cartoon.

**Print answer
here**

JUMBLE®

Unscramble these four Jumbles, one letter to each square, to form four ordinary words.

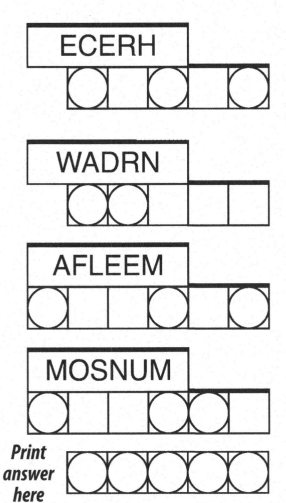

ECERH

WADRN

AFLEEM

MOSNUM

Way to work those guns!

REMEMBER THOSE WHO HAVE GIVEN ALL

THE GYM AT THE MILITARY BASE STRENGTHENED THE ---

Now arrange the circled letters to form the surprise answer, as suggested by the above cartoon.

Print answer here

JUMBLE®

Unscramble these four Jumbles, one letter to
each square, to form four ordinary words.

ZEMAA

SELYT

BABROS

DEDCLU

I'm glad I brought my
prescription goggles.

Plage
Privée

HE WORE GOGGLES IN THE
MEDITERRANEAN SO HE
COULD DO THIS.

Now arrange the circled letters to form
the surprise answer, as suggested by the
above cartoon.

Print
answer
here

" ⬭⬭⬭ " ⬭⬭⬭⬭⬭⬭⬭

JUMBLE®

Unscramble these four Jumbles, one letter to each square, to form four ordinary words.

YANOG

RONUM

DISNAL

CIKDEW

Follow me. Your seats are this way.

THE STRUGGLING ACTOR BECAME ONE WHEN HE GOT A PART-TIME JOB AS AN USHER.

Now arrange the circled letters to form the surprise answer, as suggested by the above cartoon.

Print answer here A

JUMBLE®

Unscramble these four Jumbles, one letter to each square, to form four ordinary words.

PUURS

RADAW

TTONEP

SKINTY

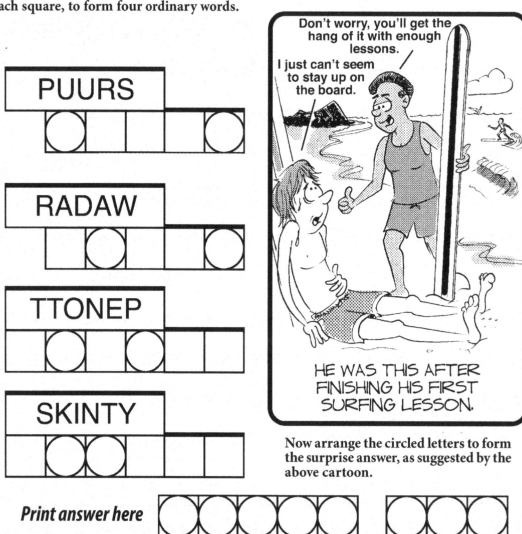

Don't worry, you'll get the hang of it with enough lessons.

I just can't seem to stay up on the board.

HE WAS THIS AFTER FINISHING HIS FIRST SURFING LESSON.

Now arrange the circled letters to form the surprise answer, as suggested by the above cartoon.

Print answer here ⬡⬡⬡⬡⬡ ⬡⬡⬡

92

JUMBLE®

Unscramble these four Jumbles, one letter to each square, to form four ordinary words.

GREEM

SAUEM

CIDOIY

CEEADD

I can't believe that you served this to me. Does anyone back there even know how to cook one of these? Did you just pull this out of the dirt and throw it on a plate? I...

WHEN HIS SWEET POTATO WAS UNDERCOOKED, HE DID THIS.

Now arrange the circled letters to form the surprise answer, as suggested by the above cartoon.

Print answer here

93

JUMBLE®

Unscramble these four Jumbles, one letter to
each square, to form four ordinary words.

RANEA

BEYRD

SMETUK

COMSHO

He's been losing
weight and has
been sluggish. I
want to fatten him
up.

THE FARMER CALLED THE
VET TO ATTEND TO THE
SICK PIG SO THAT THE PIG
COULD BECOME A ----

Now arrange the circled letters to form
the surprise answer, as suggested by the
above cartoon.

Print answer here

JUMBLE®

Unscramble these four Jumbles, one letter to
each square, to form four ordinary words.

AGGUE

NODPU

SARATY

OBYANT

Thank you for
coming in.

AFTER EXAMINING THE
CUSTOMER'S ID, THE
WAITRESS SAID, "THANK YOU
FOR YOUR ———"

Now arrange the circled letters to form
the surprise answer, as suggested by the
above cartoon.

Print answer "⬡⬡⬡⬡⬡⬡-⬡⬡⬡"
here

JUMBLE®

Unscramble these four Jumbles, one letter to
each square, to form four ordinary words.

SLEBS

RADUG

COTDEK

VOXNEC

Man! These guys always know where the fish are.

He's gonna get a bite any second.

THE TV SHOW ABOUT THE
FISHERMEN HAD A ----

Now arrange the circled letters to form
the surprise answer, as suggested by the
above cartoon.

Print answer here ◯◯◯◯ ◯◯◯◯

JUMBLE®

Unscramble these four Jumbles, one letter to each square, to form four ordinary words.

MTUSR

TOENF

FIDREF

RAMACE

We'll be on our way in no time.

He's very adept at putting up the sails.

HE BECAME SO GOOD AT PUTTING UP THE SAILS THAT HE DID THIS.

Now arrange the circled letters to form the surprise answer, as suggested by the above cartoon.

Print answer here

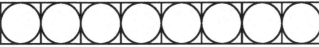

97

JUMBLE®

Unscramble these four Jumbles, one letter to each square, to form four ordinary words.

BANIC

OGAME

TANEDT

TADRSN

AFTER THE GUITARIST DONATED HIS KIDNEY, HE BECAME THIS.

Now arrange the circled letters to form the surprise answer, as suggested by the above cartoon.

Print answer here   AN

JUMBLE®

Unscramble these four Jumbles, one letter to
each square, to form four ordinary words.

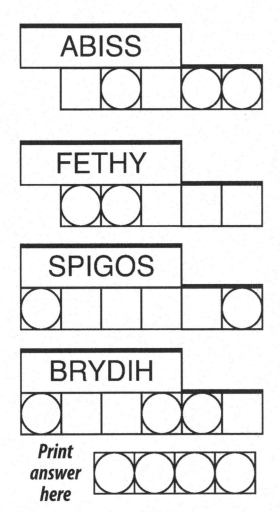

ABISS

FETHY

SPIGOS

BRYDIH

THE CHURCH SERVICE
ATOP THE MOUNTAIN
RECEIVED THIS.

Now arrange the circled letters to form
the surprise answer, as suggested by the
above cartoon.

**Print
answer
here**

JUMBLE®

Unscramble these four Jumbles, one letter to each square, to form four ordinary words.

SKIYL

EHANY

FELFUM

LUNCOM

I knew I'd win. I'm the greatest hot dog eater that has ever lived. No one can beat me. I'm the best.

WEINER CIRCLE CHAR DOG EATING CONTEST

THE WINNER OF THE HOT DOG EATING CONTEST WAS THIS.

Now arrange the circled letters to form the surprise answer, as suggested by the above cartoon.

Print answer here

OF

100

JUMBLE®

Unscramble these four Jumbles, one letter to
each square, to form four ordinary words.

KIRBN

KECER

CEANOT

RABENT

Thanks Doc.
It's feeling a
lot better.

Doc! You
gotta help
me. I can
barely move.

HOW THE
CHIROPRACTOR SAW
HIS PATIENTS.

Now arrange the circled letters to form
the surprise answer, as suggested by the
above cartoon.

Print
answer
here

◯◯◯◯ - ◯◯ - ◯◯◯◯

JUMBLE®

Unscramble these four Jumbles, one letter to
each square, to form four ordinary words.

NUCHH

CLUHM

LEYTIV

OLOINT

What about this chord
progression? Hello?
Are you even paying
attention to me?

SHE DIDN'T LIKE WORKING
ON THE NEW SONG WITH
HER BANDMATE, SO SHE
DECIDED TO ---

Now arrange the circled letters to form
the surprise answer, as suggested by the
above cartoon.

*Print
answer
here*

JUMBLE®

Unscramble these four Jumbles, one letter to each square, to form four ordinary words.

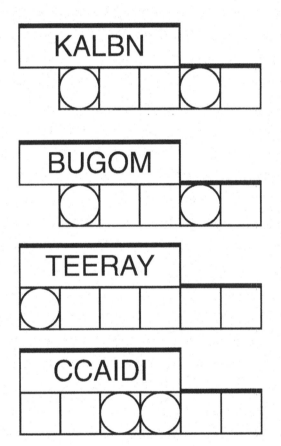

KALBN

BUGOM

TEERAY

CCAIDI

I think the Tower of London is farther up the river.

We're right here.

THE PALACE OF WESTMINSTER IS LOCATED NEAR ONE IN THE THAMES.

Now arrange the circled letters to form the surprise answer, as suggested by the above cartoon.

Print answer here A ⬡⬡⬡ ⬡⬡⬡⬡

JUMBLE®

Unscramble these four Jumbles, one letter to
each square, to form four ordinary words.

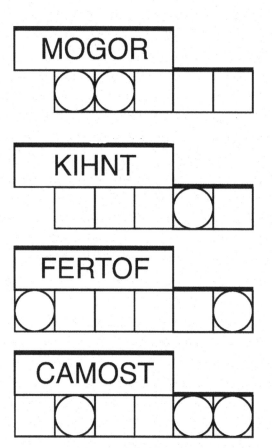

MOGOR

KIHNT

FERTOF

CAMOST

Just like
I planned.

AFTER THREE BULL'S-EYES
IN A ROW, HIS GOAL OF
WINNING AN OLYMPIC GOLD
MEDAL WAS THIS.

Now arrange the circled letters to form
the surprise answer, as suggested by the
above cartoon.

Print answer here

JUMBLE®

Unscramble these four Jumbles, one letter to each square, to form four ordinary words.

SHUIS

BANGE

SLVIEW

CINTDI

When asked about mercury levels, he replied, "No comment."

My sources say that they are perfectly healthy to eat,

THE CONVERSATION ABOUT CURRENT EVENTS WHILE THEY FISHED RESULTED IN ---

Now arrange the circled letters to form the surprise answer, as suggested by the above cartoon.

Print answer here

105

JUMBLE®

Unscramble these four Jumbles, one letter to each square, to form four ordinary words.

SMUYH

OGUBS

CAFEED

FIMRON

Don't come near my foils!

Whoa! I just wanted to know if you need any help carrying anything.

HE WAS THIS WITH HIS EXPENSIVE FENCING EQUIPMENT.

Now arrange the circled letters to form the surprise answer, as suggested by the above cartoon.

Print answer here

JUMBLE®

Unscramble these four Jumbles, one letter to
each square, to form four ordinary words.

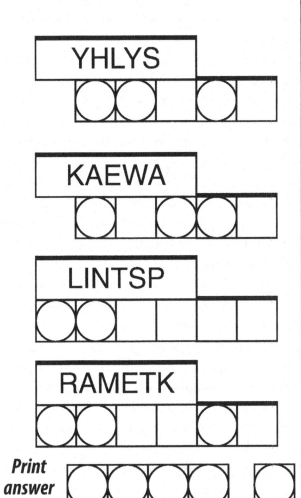

YHLYS

KAEWA

LINTSP

RAMETK

That guy
knows how
to hit the
water.

What's
his
name?

WHAT THE DIVER DIDN'T
WANT TO DO ---

Now arrange the circled letters to form
the surprise answer, as suggested by the
above cartoon.

**Print
answer
here**

JUMBLE®

Unscramble these four Jumbles, one letter to each square, to form four ordinary words.

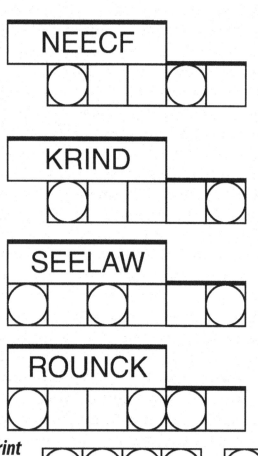

NEECF

KRIND

SEELAW

ROUNCK

WINNING THE FREE ART CLASS WAS THE ---

Now arrange the circled letters to form the surprise answer, as suggested by the above cartoon.

 THE

JUMBLE®

Unscramble these four Jumbles, one letter to each square, to form four ordinary words.

VINAA

DALUT

SCEPUR

NICRIO

How did you play, sir?

I was great off the tee.

AFTER A ROUND OF GOLF, THE BILLIONAIRE ALWAYS LEFT WITH HIS----

Now arrange the circled letters to form the surprise answer, as suggested by the above cartoon.

Print answer here

JUMBLE®

Unscramble these four Jumbles, one letter to each square, to form four ordinary words.

LHIYL

EVMOD

CETTED

NIREWY

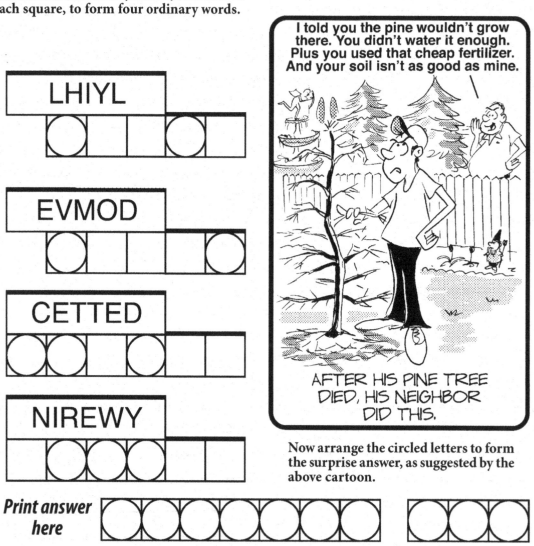

I told you the pine wouldn't grow there. You didn't water it enough. Plus you used that cheap fertilizer. And your soil isn't as good as mine.

AFTER HIS PINE TREE DIED, HIS NEIGHBOR DID THIS.

Now arrange the circled letters to form the surprise answer, as suggested by the above cartoon.

Print answer here

JUMBLE®

Unscramble these four Jumbles, one letter to
each square, to form four ordinary words.

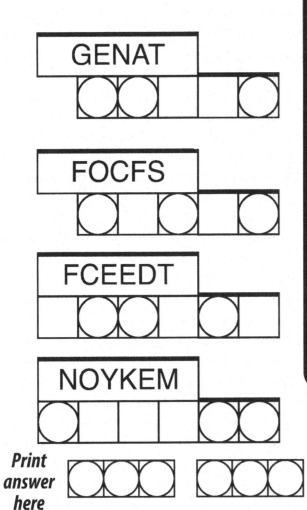

GENAT

FOCFS

FCEEDT

NOYKEM

*Print
answer
here*

I don't think you're doing a good
enough job. You need to bring in
more witnesses. You also need to
bring in an expert.

Go
away!

THE ATTORNEY SAID THIS
AFTER HER CO-WORKER
HARASSED HER ABOUT
HER WORK.

Now arrange the circled letters to form
the surprise answer, as suggested by the
above cartoon.

JUMBLE.

Unscramble these four Jumbles, one letter to each square, to form four ordinary words.

PINTU

CARNH

REALLT

UNGOHE

Oh, no! I told my wife I'd be home in time to help with dinner! Gotta go!

Give her our best.

AFTER BUMPING INTO SOME FRIENDS DURING HIS JOG, HE'D BE THIS.

Now arrange the circled letters to form the surprise answer, as suggested by the above cartoon.

Print answer here

112

JUMBLE®

Unscramble these four Jumbles, one letter to each square, to form four ordinary words.

HUVOC

THILG

KODMES

GILEBO

SAM'S SOUND SHACK

It sure is loud in here.

Buy One Get One

HIS SPEAKER BUSINESS WAS SUCCESSFUL THANKS TO ---

Now arrange the circled letters to form the surprise answer, as suggested by the above cartoon.

Print answer here

JUMBLE®

Unscramble these four Jumbles, one letter to each square, to form four ordinary words.

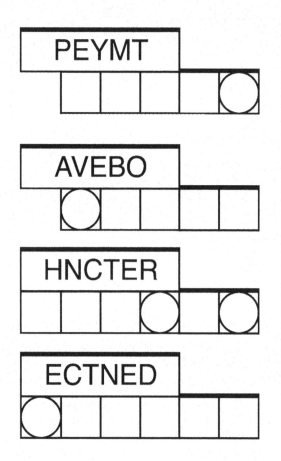

PEYMT

AVEBO

HNCTER

ECTNED

It's colder out today than I thought it would be. My fingers are numb!

No problem. I have an extra pair of gloves in the glove compartment.

HAVING AN EXTRA SET OF GLOVES IN THE GLOVE COMPARTMENT WAS ---

Now arrange the circled letters to form the surprise answer, as suggested by the above cartoon.

Print answer here

JUMBLE

Unscramble these four Jumbles, one letter to
each square, to form four ordinary words.

WREAA

HATIF

NEDLAT

MURNEB

HE OPENED HIS
BUSINESS HERE.

Now arrange the circled letters to form
the surprise answer, as suggested by the
above cartoon.

Print answer here 〇〇〇 〇〇〇〇〇

JUMBLE®

Unscramble these four Jumbles, one letter to
each square, to form four ordinary words.

ALEEG

PARMC

OSTEER

INOSOP

Print
answer
here

Shoes and
rope will be
$500 plus tax.

ALL SALES ARE FINAL.

How much?!

THE ROCK CLIMBER SAW
THESE WHEN HE WENT TO
BUY NEW CLIMBING
EQUIPMENT.

Now arrange the circled letters to form
the surprise answer, as suggested by the
above cartoon.

JUMBLE®

Unscramble these four Jumbles, one letter to
each square, to form four ordinary words.

ADDEZ

ROYIV

ORPCEP

MUSOFA

And one day I hope to have my own fleet of repair trucks.

DENNY'S PLUMBING

HIS DESIRE TO OWN THE
BIGGEST PLUMBING COMPANY
IN TOWN WAS ----

Now arrange the circled letters to form
the surprise answer, as suggested by the
above cartoon.

Print answer here **A** ⬡⬡⬡⬡⬡ ⬡⬡⬡⬡⬡⬡

117

JUMBLE®

Unscramble these four Jumbles, one letter to
each square, to form four ordinary words.

SHURC

TTHIG

LEBHOB

RAWMYL

All right!
Which one of you did
this? Or was it both
of you?

AFTER SEEING THAT HER
DOGS HAD DUG UP THE
BACK YARD, SHE
WANTED THE ---

Now arrange the circled letters to form
the surprise answer, as suggested by the
above cartoon.

Print answer " ◯◯◯◯ " ◯◯◯◯◯
here

118

JUMBLE®

Unscramble these four Jumbles, one letter to each square, to form four ordinary words.

AWREF

SLEML

NEEDOT

LEPTEL

Now, Buddy, you'll get faster as you go along!

I feel like I'm holding everybody up.

SANTA'S HELPER WAS SUFFERING FROM ----

Now arrange the circled letters to form the surprise answer, as suggested by the above cartoon.

Print answer here

☐☐☐ " ☐☐☐ " ☐☐☐☐☐☐☐

119

PUZZLE 118

JUMBLE®

Unscramble these four Jumbles, one letter to
each square, to form four ordinary words.

AFTEC

XLEEC

REVDIT

TEBNIT

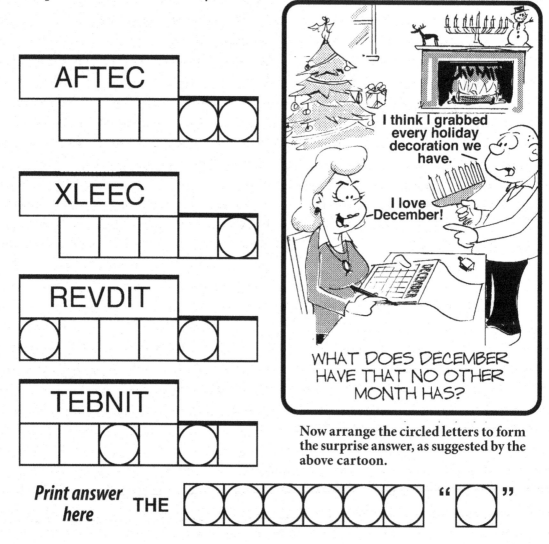

WHAT DOES DECEMBER
HAVE THAT NO OTHER
MONTH HAS?

Now arrange the circled letters to form
the surprise answer, as suggested by the
above cartoon.

Print answer here THE ◯◯◯◯◯◯ "◯"

120

JUMBLE®

Unscramble these four Jumbles, one letter to
each square, to form four ordinary words.

RIKEH

DOORE

OVDECI

ALODDE

What are they doing?

Watch this!

Eww! They're stinking up the place!

THE SKUNK
HOODLUMS ----

Now arrange the circled letters to form
the surprise answer, as suggested by the
above cartoon.

Print answer here " ◯◯◯◯◯ " ◯◯◯◯◯

JUMBLE®

Unscramble these four Jumbles, one letter to each square, to form four ordinary words.

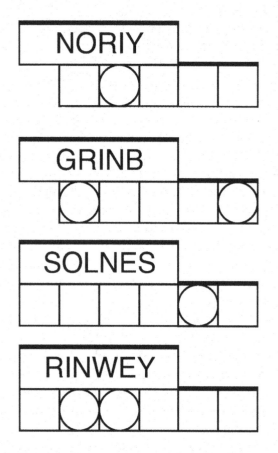

NORIY

GRINB

SOLNES

RINWEY

HIS JOB AT THE MINE WAS AND WASN'T ———

Now arrange the circled letters to form the surprise answer, as suggested by the above cartoon.

Print answer here

JUMBLE®

Unscramble these four Jumbles, one letter to
each square, to form four ordinary words.

EGAIL

ONNIU

DURRED

VAWIRE

Good luck
and thanks
for Jumbling!

I'm a
big fan.

WIN AN
ORIGINAL
JUMBLE
CARTOON !

THE JUMBLE
ARTIST'S CARTOON
IS A ----

Now arrange the circled letters to form
the surprise answer, as suggested by the
above cartoon.

Print
answer
here

JUMBLE®

Unscramble these four Jumbles, one letter to
each square, to form four ordinary words.

TOPIV

CRUNH

TARLOM

SINOCA

We unanimously, absolutely
find the defendant completely
guilty!

THE JURY
REACHED ITS
DECISION WITH ----

Now arrange the circled letters to form
the surprise answer, as suggested by the
above cartoon.

**Print answer
here**

JUMBLE®

Unscramble these four Jumbles, one letter to
each square, to form four ordinary words.

DUNPO

RIMSK

PELTIR

SACHWE

THE MODEL BOATS
WERE READY
TO ---

Now arrange the circled letters to form
the surprise answer, as suggested by the
above cartoon.

Print
answer
here

125

PUZZLE 124

JUMBLE®

Unscramble these four Jumbles, one letter to each square, to form four ordinary words.

MIPRP

LIRGL

HOPNOT

RIFFAM

WHEN IT CAME TO WHICH SANDALS SHE WANTED TO BUY, THE CUSTOMER KEPT ---

Now arrange the circled letters to form the surprise answer, as suggested by the above cartoon.

Print answer here: ◯◯◯◯ - ◯◯◯◯◯◯◯◯◯

126

JUMBLE®

Unscramble these four Jumbles, one letter to each square, to form four ordinary words.

FITHS

NOWEM

CARPIY

RELYCE

Let's make it so we go over there.

Let me take charge and we'll go faster.

THE BALLOON WAS ASCENDING PERFECTLY, BUT THE SQUABBLING OPERATORS WERE GOING ———

Now arrange the circled letters to form the surprise answer, as suggested by the above cartoon.

Print answer here

JUMBLE®

Unscramble these four Jumbles, one letter to each square, to form four ordinary words.

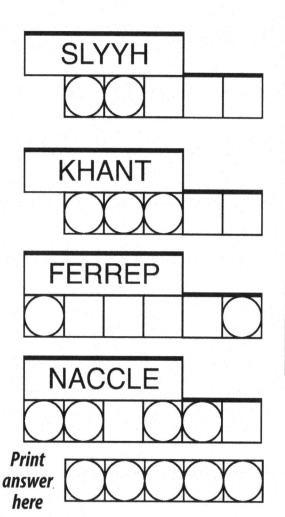

SLYYH

KHANT

FERREP

NACCLE

Print answer here

You'll be HOOKED on our fish!

That's perfect! People will love it.

THE FISH MARKET'S NEW SLOGAN WAS A ---

Now arrange the circled letters to form the surprise answer, as suggested by the above cartoon.

128

JUMBLE®

Unscramble these four Jumbles, one letter to
each square, to form four ordinary words.

PEMUL

TAABE

ANESKY

TINCSH

You've got some recovery time ahead of you.

I'll be back in the office one, maybe two weeks tops.

THE DOCTOR WOULD
RECOVER FROM HIS INJURIES
IF HE COULD ----

Now arrange the circled letters to form
the surprise answer, as suggested by the
above cartoon.

Print answer here ⬡⬡ ⬡⬡⬡⬡⬡⬡⬡

129

JUMBLE®

Unscramble these four Jumbles, one letter to each square, to form four ordinary words.

FRAWH

TUMOH

GLEPED

NOYRED

Heidi, you are making it work today!

It's all in the walk, Tim.

HEIDI KLUM WAS WORKING THE MINUTE SHE STEPPED OFF THE PLANE BECAUSE SHE WAS———

Now arrange the circled letters to form the surprise answer, as suggested by the above cartoon.

Print answer here   A

JUMBLE®

Unscramble these four Jumbles, one letter to each square, to form four ordinary words.

RREVI

DEEWG

DRANTS

COTREK

I'm going to check this out.

BIG OLD BANK AND TRUST

New Customers Receive 5% Return!

AFTER SEEING HOW MUCH THE BANK'S SAVINGS ACCOUNTS EARNED, HE WAS ----

Now arrange the circled letters to form the surprise answer, as suggested by the above cartoon.

Print answer here

131

JUMBLE®

Unscramble these four Jumbles, one letter to each square, to form four ordinary words.

SOREA

WOYHD

LEYWOL

EPCOIT

What a sight! So much ocean to explore.

MAGELLAN SET OUT TO CIRCUMNAVIGATE THE GLOBE AND WAS ABLE TO ---

Now arrange the circled letters to form the surprise answer, as suggested by the above cartoon.

Print answer here

" ☐☐☐ " ☐☐☐ ☐☐☐☐☐

132

JUMBLE®

Unscramble these four Jumbles, one letter to each square, to form four ordinary words.

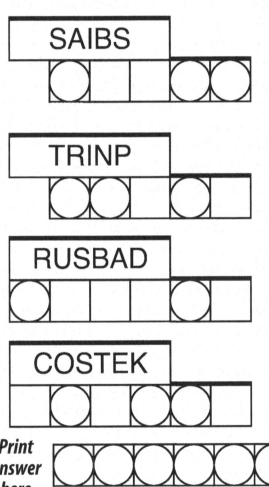

SAIBS

TRINP

RUSBAD

COSTEK

I had to get out of there. That bird guy was driving me crazy.

WHEN THE GUARDS AT ALCATRAZ NEEDED A REST, THEY TOOK A - - - -

Now arrange the circled letters to form the surprise answer, as suggested by the above cartoon.

Print answer here

PUZZLE
132

JUMBLE®

Unscramble these four Jumbles, one letter to each square, to form four ordinary words.

WETKA

VALEE

RODPOY

TOBNUT

Wow! These are so much clearer.

It's a much better prescription and style for you.

WHEN SHE GOT NEW GLASSES, SHE ---

Now arrange the circled letters to form the surprise answer, as suggested by the above cartoon.

Print answer here

134

JUMBLE®

Unscramble these four Jumbles, one letter to
each square, to form four ordinary words.

EDDDA

SLELP

NOCPAY

TURBET

That will be $26.50.

Here. Use this card. I'll need these diapers in 11 days.

THE EXPECTANT MOTHER
TIED EVERYTHING
TO HER ---

Now arrange the circled letters to form
the surprise answer, as suggested by the
above cartoon.

Print answer here ⃝⃝⃝ ⃝⃝⃝⃝

JUMBLE

Unscramble these four Jumbles, one letter to each square, to form four ordinary words.

SCURT

MFIYL

MOCNOM

TEREJS

I'm so happy. I can't stop crying.

It's just so beautiful!

WHAT SHE HAD WHEN SHE SAW HER WEDDING CAKE.

Now arrange the circled letters to form the surprise answer, as suggested by the above cartoon.

Print answer here

" ⬡⬡⬡⬡⬡ "   ⬡⬡   ⬡⬡⬡

JUMBLE®

Unscramble these four Jumbles, one letter to each square, to form four ordinary words.

WRIEP

NOION

SEBHUL

RUBUNA

I'd love to take it on a short trip.

As you wish. It's your boat.

THE BILLIONAIRE WAS ABLE TO ENJOY THE NEW YACHT THANKS TO ---

Now arrange the circled letters to form the surprise answer, as suggested by the above cartoon.

Print answer here

137

JUMBLE®

Unscramble these four Jumbles, one letter to
each square, to form four ordinary words.

NEYPN

KHINT

CLAOLE

NEBURK

I'm really
going to miss
you two.

I'll update
you on
Facebook.

I'll call
you.

WHEN THE MASSEUSE
LEFT HER JOB, THEY
WANTED HER TO ---

Now arrange the circled letters to form
the surprise answer, as suggested by the
above cartoon.

Print
answer
here

JUMBLE®

Unscramble these four Jumbles, one letter to
each square, to form four ordinary words.

SIBAC

PATRA

RIPREM

NITMUY

I'm glad our parties could work together on this bill.

There should only be one party. The American party.

I'll sign this right away.

IF POLITICIANS EVER TRULY
STARTED TO WORK
TOGETHER, THEN IT
WOULD BE ----

Now arrange the circled letters to form
the surprise answer, as suggested by the
above cartoon.

Print answer here " ⃝⃝⃝ " - ⃝⃝⃝⃝⃝⃝⃝⃝⃝

JUMBLE®

Unscramble these four Jumbles, one letter to each square, to form four ordinary words.

SLACH

RUTOC

BORREK

SIGTED

I'll return to the marina. There's a medical station there.

I feel awful.

WHEN SHE GOT SICK AFTER THEY SET SAIL, HE NEEDED TO GET----

Now arrange the circled letters to form the surprise answer, as suggested by the above cartoon.

Print answer here

⬡⬡⬡⬡ ⬡⬡ ⬡⬡⬡ "⬡⬡⬡"

JUMBLE

Unscramble these four Jumbles, one letter to each square, to form four ordinary words.

This is what put you through college.

EVUEN

ROYLG

UCONIS

VITACE

RUNNING THE CREMATION SOCIETY MADE IT POSSIBLE FOR HIM TO ---

Now arrange the circled letters to form the surprise answer, as suggested by the above cartoon.

Print answer here " ◯◯◯ " ◯   ◯◯◯◯◯◯◯

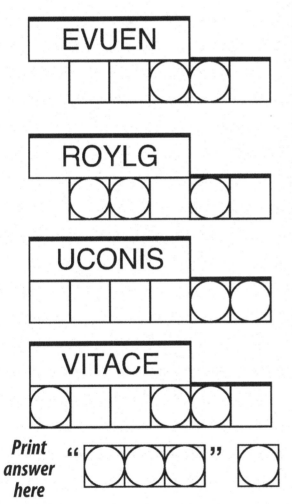

JUMBLE®

Unscramble these four Jumbles, one letter to each square, to form four ordinary words.

TRAGF

GEAAD

FADEET

FOHODE

This is the ___ best sandwich I've ever tasted.

I'm getting full.

AFTER HIKING DOWN TO THE BOTTOM OF THE GRAND CANYON, THEY ———

Now arrange the circled letters to form the surprise answer, as suggested by the above cartoon.

Print answer here

142

JUMBLE®

Unscramble these four Jumbles, one letter to
each square, to form four ordinary words.

WARLT

TOBIR

NEYGAC

LUPTIP

Your kids
are going to
contest this
if you give
it all away.

Well, I
really
want to
give this a
shot.

HE WASN'T SURE IF HE
COULD GIVE ALL HIS
FORTUNE TO CHARITY
UPON HIS DEATH,
BUT HE WAS ----

Now arrange the circled letters to form
the surprise answer, as suggested by the
above cartoon.

Print
answer
here

JUMBLE®

Unscramble these four Jumbles, one letter to
each square, to form four ordinary words.

MEOGA

KOBER

UNSAAE

RIHTEM

Do you have
a sugar cube
I could
borrow?

Of course.
Anything
for you.

11   12

THE HORSES IN THE
BARN WERE ---

Now arrange the circled letters to form
the surprise answer, as suggested by the
above cartoon.

Print answer " ◯◯◯◯◯ - ◯◯◯◯ "
here

JUMBLE®

Unscramble these four Jumbles, one letter to each square, to form four ordinary words.

INVEX

GUWNS

LEFNOY

SAMPIH

This street really needed the rehab.

Looks great.

ALL THE RECENT CONSTRUCTION WAS TURNING THE STREET INTO ---

Now arrange the circled letters to form the surprise answer, as suggested by the above cartoon.

Print answer here AN " ◯◯◯ - ◯◯◯ "

145

JUMBLE®

Unscramble these four Jumbles, one letter to each square, to form four ordinary words.

NCEFE

NIDRK

ROPRAL

SYMCIT

THEY NEEDED ONE WHEN THEY FILMED THE MOVIE'S BANK ROBBERY SCENE.

Now arrange the circled letters to form the surprise answer, as suggested by the above cartoon.

Print answer here

A

JUMBLE®

Unscramble these four Jumbles, one letter to
each square, to form four ordinary words.

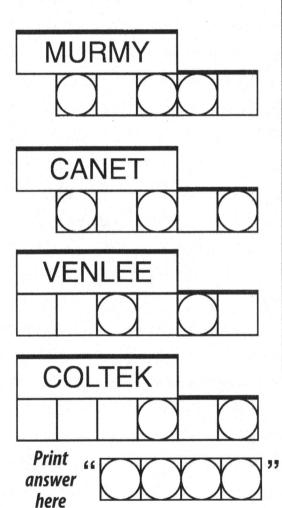

MURMY

CANET

VENLEE

COLTEK

Well, hello,
gorgeous! My
name's Sam.

Hello to you,
Sam. I'm Alice.
What are you
doing for
dinner?

GROUND

LOVE AT FIRST SIGHT
TURNED THE BUTCHER
SHOP INTO A ---

Now arrange the circled letters to form
the surprise answer, as suggested by the
above cartoon.

**Print
answer
here** " ⬡⬡⬡⬡ " ⬡⬡⬡⬡⬡⬡⬡

JUMBLE®

Unscramble these four Jumbles, one letter to each square, to form four ordinary words.

FETHI

TURMS

VEGRON

YADNIT

You'll have your day.

Let me hear your Stewie voice.

Cheers!

WHEN THE ACTORS AND ACTRESSES CELEBRATED THEIR OSCAR AWARD WINS, IT WAS A – – – –

Now arrange the circled letters to form the surprise answer, as suggested by the above cartoon.

Print answer here

JUMBLE®

Unscramble these four Jumbles, one letter to each square, to form four ordinary words.

UQTIL

LOCTU

ORPNEV

NEDYOK

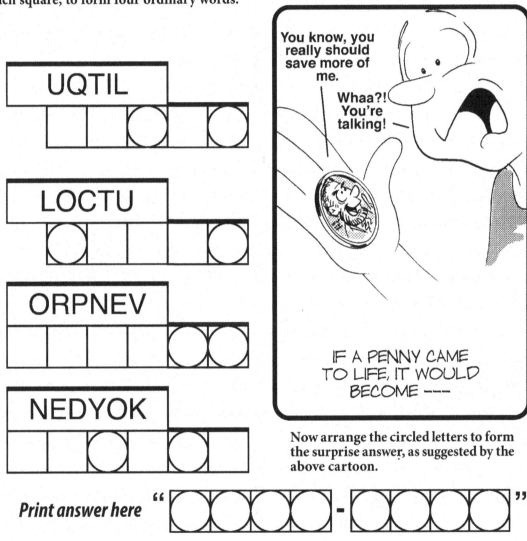

You know, you really should save more of me.

Whaa?! You're talking!

IF A PENNY CAME TO LIFE, IT WOULD BECOME ----

Now arrange the circled letters to form the surprise answer, as suggested by the above cartoon.

Print answer here "◯◯◯◯ - ◯◯◯◯"

JUMBLE®

Unscramble these four Jumbles, one letter to each square, to form four ordinary words.

CLOBK

ROYIV

GEDEER

DOHSUL

You look hot. Would you like a drink?

Thanks! This deck should be really strong.

THE CARPENTER HAD A ----

Now arrange the circled letters to form the surprise answer, as suggested by the above cartoon.

Print answer here

⬡⬡⬡⬡ ⬡⬡⬡⬡⬡

JUMBLE®

Unscramble these four Jumbles, one letter to each square, to form four ordinary words.

BAEDI

TRADY

RIPTOF

EFTCED

Would you take this watch? It should cover what I owe you.

I already have a watch.

WHEN HE DIDN'T HAVE ENOUGH MONEY TO PAY THE TAXI DRIVER, HE OFFERED A ---

Now arrange the circled letters to form the surprise answer, as suggested by the above cartoon.

Print answer here " ☐☐☐☐☐ " ☐☐☐☐☐☐

JUMBLE®

Unscramble these four Jumbles, one letter to each square, to form four ordinary words.

LAVEV

CONHA

SINTIS

CITDUN

Don't bother struggling. I have you in my trance.

I can't move.

HER ATTEMPT TO GET AWAY FROM DRACULA WAS GOING TO BE ----

Now arrange the circled letters to form the surprise answer, as suggested by the above cartoon.

Print answer here ⬡⬡ " ⬡⬡⬡⬡ "

152

JUMBLE®

Unscramble these four Jumbles, one letter to each square, to form four ordinary words.

NADTS

TAIRO

RUHOYL

CETEND

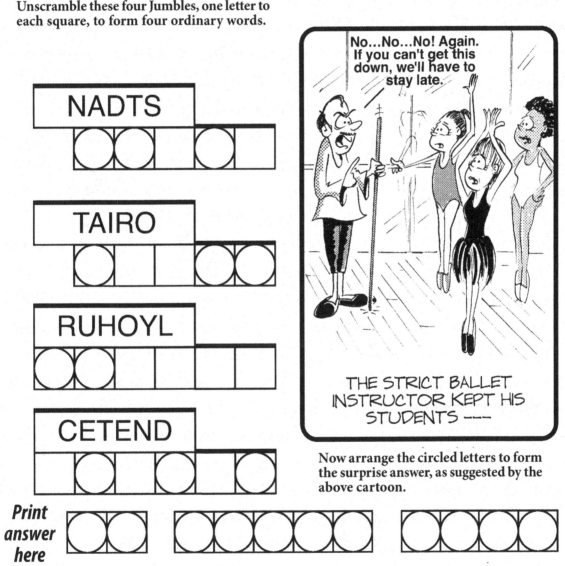

No...No...No! Again. If you can't get this down, we'll have to stay late.

THE STRICT BALLET INSTRUCTOR KEPT HIS STUDENTS ----

Now arrange the circled letters to form the surprise answer, as suggested by the above cartoon.

Print answer here

153

JUMBLE®

Unscramble these four Jumbles, one letter to
each square, to form four ordinary words.

VAHCO

NORPE

GLEEDU

CAIDOZ

FINISH

Sorry to have
broken your
winning streak.

That's ok. I
really
enjoyed
myself out
there today.

AFTER FIVE MARATHON
VICTORIES IN A ROW, HE
LOST...BUT HE DIDN'T
MIND...HE'D ———

Now arrange the circled letters to form
the surprise answer, as suggested by the
above cartoon.

Print
answer
here

PUZZLE 153

JUMBLE®

Unscramble these four Jumbles, one letter to each square, to form four ordinary words.

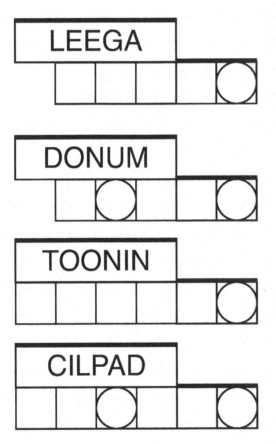

LEEGA

DONUM

TOONIN

CILPAD

Wow! You just can't miss today.

I guess I'm a natural.

THE ZOMBIE WAS SUCH A GOOD ARCHER BECAUSE HIS AIM WAS ---

Now arrange the circled letters to form the surprise answer, as suggested by the above cartoon.

Print answer here ◯◯◯◯ ◯◯

155

JUMBLE®

Unscramble these four Jumbles, one letter to
each square, to form four ordinary words.

VEARG

NUCHH

RIHYTT

ALBBEB

I wish I had some gloves.

I can't feel my fingers.

WHEN THEY VISITED
THE CAPITAL OF GERMANY
IN THE FRIGID WEATHER,
THEY VISITED ----

Now arrange the circled letters to form
the surprise answer, as suggested by the
above cartoon.

Print answer here " ☐☐☐☐☐ - ☐☐☐ "

156

JUMBLE®

Unscramble these four Jumbles, one letter to
each square, to form four ordinary words.

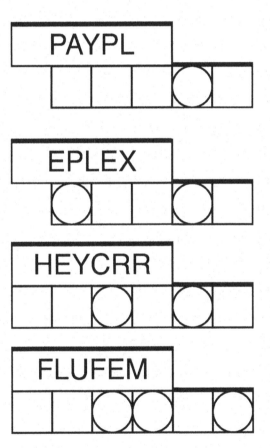

PAYPL

EPLEX

HEYCRR

FLUFEM

MASSAGE MASTER
30 min. intro. -$50
60 min. Full Body- $100

Will this cover
a 30-minute
massage?

Why, yes.
That will
cover it.

$50 OFF

30 min.
for $50

WHEN SHE ASKED IF SHE
COULD USE THE SPA
COUPON FOR A MASSAGE,
THEY SAID ----

Now arrange the circled letters to form
the surprise answer, as suggested by the
above cartoon.

Print answer here

JUMBLE®

Unscramble these four Jumbles, one letter to
each square, to form four ordinary words.

YUCIJ

ELBAZ

MILPEP

RIVUTE

NOBEL'S PIZZERIA

CHEESE SAUSAGE WORKS

VOTED
City's
Best
Slice!

This is the
best, Alfredo!

That's what
they say.

THE PIZZA MAKER'S
AWARD-WINNING
SLICE WON A ----

Now arrange the circled letters to form
the surprise answer, as suggested by the
above cartoon.

Print
answer
here

" ⬡⬡⬡⬡⬡ " ⬡⬡⬡⬡⬡

JUMBLE®

Unscramble these four Jumbles, one letter to
each square, to form four ordinary words.

SOINB

LATTO

VIREEV

LIMFAY

SHE OPENED HER FLOWER
SHOP WHEN SHE WAS IN HER
70s BECAUSE SHE WAS A ----

Now arrange the circled letters to form
the surprise answer, as suggested by the
above cartoon.

**Print
answer
here**

JUMBLE®

Unscramble these four Jumbles, one letter to each square, to form four ordinary words.

RIHEK
◻️◯◻️◯◻️

INAGA
◯◯◻️◯

LODONE
◯◻️◻️◯◯◻️

PAMCIT
◻️◯◻️◯◻️◻️

I knew I could get Tom Hanks to run again.

THE MOVIE ABOUT THE WINNER OF THE MARATHON FEATURED A ---

Now arrange the circled letters to form the surprise answer, as suggested by the above cartoon.

Print answer here ◻️◯◯◯◯◯◯◯ ◻️◯◯◯

JUMBLE®

Unscramble these four Jumbles, one letter to each square, to form four ordinary words.

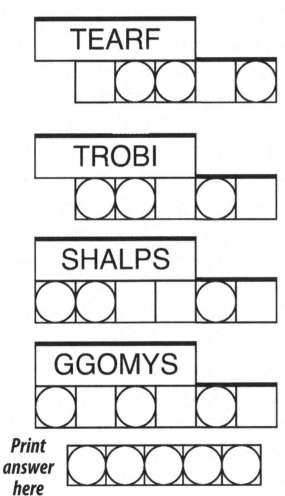

TEARF

TROBI

SHALPS

GGOMYS

This is our best seller. Looks like the real thing.

UNCLE FUN

Ewww! That's nasty!

THE STORE OWNER'S FAKE VOMIT AND OTHER DIS-GUSTING NOVELTIES RESULTED IN ----

Now arrange the circled letters to form the surprise answer, as suggested by the above cartoon.

Print answer here

161

JUMBLE®

Unscramble these four Jumbles, one letter to each square, to form four ordinary words.

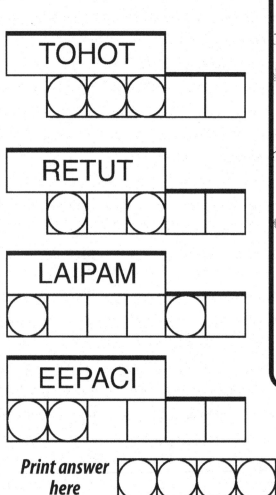

TOHOT

RETUT

LAIPAM

EEPACI

This traffic is ridiculous! I'm going to miss my flight.

THE CAPTAIN OF THE PLANE WAS LATE FOR WORK AFTER SPENDING TOO MUCH TIME AS AN ----

Now arrange the circled letters to form the surprise answer, as suggested by the above cartoon.

Print answer here

162

JUMBLE®

WORKOUT

CHALLENGER PUZZLES

JUMBLE®

Unscramble these six Jumbles, one letter to each square, to form six ordinary words.

APUORR

LNMIEG

RYOWTH

AILSDN

ASIRAF

LWUATN

Are you the guy who does the Jumble cartoons?

Yes I am! Do you Jumble?

HOW JEFF KNUREK KILLS TIME WHILE WAITING IN LINE AT THE BANK.

Now arrange the circled letters to form the surprise answer, as suggested by the above cartoon.

Print answer here

164

JUMBLE®

Unscramble these six Jumbles, one letter to each square, to form six ordinary words.

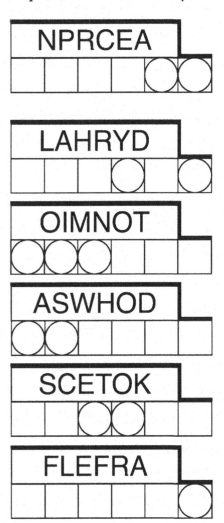

NPRCEA

LAHRYD

OIMNOT

ASWHOD

SCETOK

FLEFRA

That's a funny drawing.

Look, she's tweeting!

THE ARTISTS' STAGE PERFORMANCE WAS A ---

Now arrange the circled letters to form the surprise answer, as suggested by the above cartoon.

Print answer here

JUMBLE®

Unscramble these six Jumbles, one letter to each square, to form six ordinary words.

OTOTAT

RWTAHM

LFOEWL

NSIEGU

DIOIEN

NFEULG

Shouldn't he be at the aquarium?

He's already taken a bite out of my chip stack.

He's not so great!

THE CARD SHARK ATTRACTED SO MUCH ATTENTION BECAUSE HE WAS A ---

Now arrange the circled letters to form the surprise answer, as suggested by the above cartoon.

Print answer here

⬡⬡⬡⬡⬡ ⬡⬡⬡⬡ ⬡⬡ ⬡⬡⬡⬡⬡⬡

JUMBLE®

Unscramble these six Jumbles, one letter to each square, to form six ordinary words.

PEHANP

RRLYBU

HIBPOS

REONVP

ACGELN

HAROTU

...and we'd listen to the Lone Ranger on the radio. And I once saw the Andrews Sisters with Bob Hope...

Today it's flat screens, Lady Gaga, and iPhones.

WHAT THE GRANDFATHER TALKED ABOUT WHEN DESCRIBING THE GOOD OLD DAYS.

Now arrange the circled letters to form the surprise answer, as suggested by the above cartoon.

Print answer here

" ◯◯◯ " ◯◯◯◯◯◯◯◯

167

JUMBLE®

Unscramble these six Jumbles, one letter to each square, to form six ordinary words.

GEJORG

TEBAYR

LFEADW

WELYEA

INMIGN

OSRYTM

You're still out here?
You must be exhausted.

GARDENING
ALL DAY RESULTED
IN HER ---

Now arrange the circled letters to form the surprise answer, as suggested by the above cartoon.

Print answer here

JUMBLE

Unscramble these six Jumbles, one letter to
each square, to form six ordinary words.

SFOYTR

WTOHNR

LEREVC

HENITZ

LUONDT

YESPEL

I told you that
you should have
gone right back
there.

Don't worry.
I'm still hoping
we'll be able to
recover some
time.

TAKING A LEFT
AT THE LAST
INTERSECTION
WAS A ---

Now arrange the circled letters to form
the surprise answer, as suggested by
the above cartoon.

Print answer here

169

JUMBLE®

Unscramble these six Jumbles, one letter to each square, to form six ordinary words.

GABNIK

RROYAM

DLUEGS

TWOIUT

RCEYLG

REAACM

THE DISPUTE AT THE AIRPORT RESULTED IN ---

Now arrange the circled letters to form the surprise answer, as suggested by the above cartoon.

Print answer here

JUMBLE®

Unscramble these six Jumbles, one letter to
each square, to form six ordinary words.

SEUFRE

MOLCNU

LHIWEA

NIRIGA

OUIRST

EADSYW

And they said
our design was
nuts. We sure
showed them
how to go
above and
beyond.

THEY WERE ABLE TO WIN
THE HOT-AIR BALLOON
COMPETITION BECAUSE
THEY ---

Now arrange the circled letters to form
the surprise answer, as suggested by
the above cartoon.

Print answer here

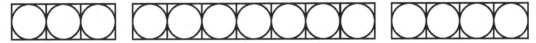

171

JUMBLE®

Unscramble these six Jumbles, one letter to each square, to form six ordinary words.

ONDZIG

CTAHHT

ARISNP

DILMED

LIVINO

GERRTE

That little Pelé is amazing. With as much as he practices, it's no surprise he's as good as he is.

BECOMING THE WORLD'S GREATEST SOCCER PLAYER WAS THIS.

Now arrange the circled letters to form the surprise answer, as suggested by the above cartoon.

Print answer here

172

JUMBLE®

Unscramble these six Jumbles, one letter to each square, to form six ordinary words.

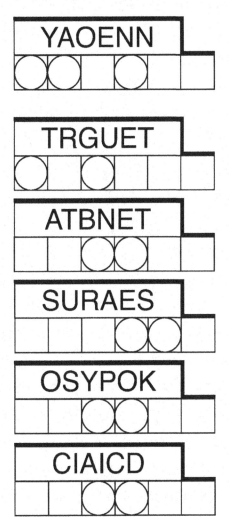

YAOENN

TRGUET

ATBNET

SURAES

OSYPOK

CIAICD

One day I'm going to circumnavigate the world.

So what are you waiting for? Do it.

This really needs some spice.

MAGELLAN PROBABLY IMAGINED HIMSELF CIRCLING THE GLOBE YEARS BEFORE HE FINALLY----

Now arrange the circled letters to form the surprise answer, as suggested by the above cartoon.

Print answer here

JUMBLE®

Unscramble these six Jumbles, one letter to each square, to form six ordinary words.

SWARLP

CAUKNP

CEODIV

PABTEU

KOECST

SCAIOF

We'll have to cancel today's events.

Oh my!

THE CHURCH WITH THE PLUMBING PROBLEMS WAS THIS.

Now arrange the circled letters to form the surprise answer, as suggested by the above cartoon.

Print answer here

174

JUMBLE®

Unscramble these six Jumbles, one letter to
each square, to form six ordinary words.

FRAIMF

TEILBG

RLUUNY

WASRLP

TSTOPY

ADRREH

Sly, no one
knows who
you are.

This is MY movie! If
I'm not in it, it's not
gonna fly.

I'm thinking
Redford is
perfect for this
part.

ROCKY
by
Sylvester
Stallone

PRODUCERS DIDN'T WANT
SYLVESTER STALLONE TO
STAR IN "ROCKY,"
SO HE ----

Now arrange the circled letters to form
the surprise answer, as suggested by
the above cartoon.

Print answer here

JUMBLE®

Unscramble these six Jumbles, one letter to each square, to form six ordinary words.

TISCTH

DIFLDE

THWROG

VUNAEE

NISRGT

DIUTOS

I really love this new flat-screen.

dic·tion·ar·y
/ dikSHa nerē/
A book that lists the words of a language in alphabetical order and gives their meaning, or

He sure was sharp.

THE DOCUMENTARY ABOUT DICTIONARY-MAKER NOAH WEBSTER WAS IN ----

Now arrange the circled letters to form the surprise answer, as suggested by the above cartoon.

Print answer here

176

JUMBLE®

Unscramble these six Jumbles, one letter to each square, to form six ordinary words.

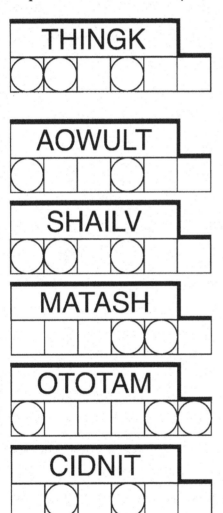

THINGK

AOWULT

SHAILV

MATASH

OTOTAM

CIDNIT

J&D MOVING
We barely break anything.

Traffic is always a nightmare, and the cost is killing me!

HIS COMMUTE TO WORK WAS THIS.

Now arrange the circled letters to form the surprise answer, as suggested by the above cartoon.

Print answer here

 A

JUMBLE®

Unscramble these six Jumbles, one letter to
each square, to form six ordinary words.

GDDEER

CUYCOP

RONFEZ

OSLICA

FALLUW

TECNIE

I'm glad you all could make it.

Wouldn't miss it.

You forgot your hair, Bill.

WHEN HE SAT AROUND
THE CAMPFIRE WITH HIS
BUDDIES, HE WAS
WITH HIS ---

Now arrange the circled letters to form
the surprise answer, as suggested by
the above cartoon.

Print answer here

178

JUMBLE®

Unscramble these six Jumbles, one letter to each square, to form six ordinary words.

WOTDAR

USMELS

EATLYL

REWITR

RREOPP

PAIUTO

People will enjoy this statue for years to come.

You can count on it.

HANS WILSDORF
1881-1960

WHEN THEY PUT A WRISTWATCH ON THE STATUE, ---

Now arrange the circled letters to form the surprise answer, as suggested by the above cartoon.

Print answer here

JUMBLE®

Unscramble these six Jumbles, one letter to each square, to form six ordinary words.

IDARAF

BHLUEM

TGONUI

ATHEHL

CRIEEF

DIOYTD

I think Little Mickey is going to be a star one day.

MANTLE

HE WAS GOOD AT BASEBALL – – –

Now arrange the circled letters to form the surprise answer, as suggested by the above cartoon.

Print answer here

180

JUMBLE®

Unscramble these six Jumbles, one letter to each square, to form six ordinary words.

LABDAL

THEGLN

SNITIS

SLWARP

YANMIF

ADNMET

MARY'S SHEEP FARM

He's beautiful. I can't wait to show him off around town.

WHEN HER SHEEP GAVE BIRTH, MARY ---

Now arrange the circled letters to form the surprise answer, as suggested by the above cartoon.

Print answer here

181

JUMBLE

Unscramble these six Jumbles, one letter to each square, to form six ordinary words.

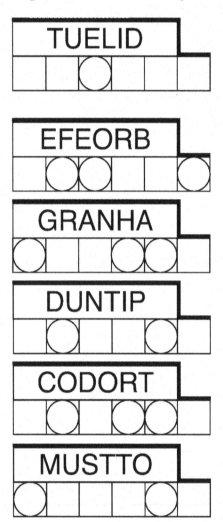

TUELID

EFEORB

GRANHA

DUNTIP

CODORT

MUSTTO

Maybe we can get together for dinner sometime.

I think you're going to be sitting on the bench alone.

THE NBA PLAYER DIDN'T STAND A CHANCE WITH THE WNBA PLAYER BECAUSE SHE WAS THIS.

Now arrange the circled letters to form the surprise answer, as suggested by the above cartoon.

Print answer here

JUMBLE®

Unscramble these six Jumbles, one letter to each square, to form six ordinary words.

HOSRCC

RILDAZ

TEHIRE

TRAYNP

ANGIGZ

LUBIYS

Wow! He's a natural.

I'm glad he's on our team.

MEN'S LEA
NIGHT
WEDNESD

HE STARTED
BOWLING BECAUSE HE
THOUGHT
IT WOULD BE THIS.

Now arrange the circled letters to form the surprise answer, as suggested by the above cartoon.

Print answer here

ANSWERS

1. **Jumbles:** BOOTH THUMP SHRIMP BOTTLE
   Answer: She thought her subway ride was this—THE PITS

2. **Jumbles:** SKIMP TAUNT THROAT MUFFIN
   Answer: The skunk would probably get fired from her job because she—STUNK AT IT

3. **Jumbles:** BENCH TARDY FIASCO DRENCH
   Answer: It didn't take long for Richard Starkey's parents to realize he was going to—BE A "STARR"

4. **Jumbles:** QUEEN TEMPO PROFIT INDUCT
   Answer: Starting construction without the proper paperwork was—NOT PERMITTED

5. **Jumbles:** ABHOR SUSHI MADCAP ENROLL
   Answer: Putting a 30-second time limit on today's puzzle would cause you to do this—SCRAMBLE

6. **Jumbles:** GUAVA ICING GLADLY AGENCY
   Answer: Loading the luggage for their vacation was a chore because of all the—LUGGING

7. **Jumbles:** ALPHA MURKY KETTLE WEAKEN
   Answer: With the high price of gas, a full tank can lead to—AN EMPTY WALLET

8. **Jumbles:** SILKY THICK BAFFLE PUDDLE
   Answer: When they were upgraded at check-in, they considered it this—A "SUITE" DEAL

9. **Jumbles:** THUMB SIXTY PRETTY RUDDER
   Answer: Their day at the beach did this—SUITED THEM

10. **Jumbles:** DUNCE ROBOT CAVORT DOUBLE
    Answer: After a few days of vacationing at the beach, they were this—BURNT OUT

11. **Jumbles:** FLUTE FLOOD BALLET BEHAVE
    Answer: They bought the subdivision parcel because they thought it had this—A LOT OF VALUE

12. **Jumbles:** WORRY HONOR GALLEY DIVEST
    Answer: His new electric car was a—"VOLTS WAGON"

13. **Jumbles:** MATCH UNCLE VISION LIZARD
    Answer: The Minneapolis beverage maker hoped to have a big success with this—"MINI SODA"

14. **Jumbles:** CLIMB DRAFT GOSSIP GOALIE
    Answer: The Olympic runner liked to remember the—GOOD TIMES

15. **Jumbles:** WEAVE AWAKE GARLIC SHODDY
    Answer: He couldn't keep the fact that he was a zombie a secret because he was a—DEAD GIVEAWAY

16. **Jumbles:** HUSKY AGING DROWSY ROBBER
    Answer: Founded in 1898, Frank Seiberling's tire and rubber company has had many—GOOD YEARS

17. **Jumbles:** CHORD WORLD REMOVE FEEBLE
    Answer: Being shot at by the hunters put the duck in this—A "FOWL" MOOD

18. **Jumbles:** HOBBY JUDGE FORBID IRONIC
    Answer: How she felt after spraying the lawn for insects—GRUBBY

19. **Jumbles:** POLKA ANNEX PIGLET ABSORB
    Answer: His explanation of how the famous crack formed did this—RANG A BELL

20. **Jumbles:** SHIFT CLOWN CURBED SHAKEN
    Answer: The photography teacher had everything he needed, but his students—LACKED FOCUS

21. **Jumbles:** BRAVO OMEGA DROWSY CHERUB
    Answer: When they went to New York City, they saw these—BURROS

22. **Jumbles:** KAZOO PRONE IMPALA ABATED
    Answer: The librarian was very clear about how she felt because she was—AN OPEN BOOK

23. **Jumbles:** FORGO YIELD MAGPIE SAVANT
    Answer: If they wanted to have everything packed up on time, they'd need to—GET A MOVE ON

24. **Jumbles:** RHYME ELDER MOOLAH URGING
    Answer: The sale at the nursery turned the customer into a—HEDGE HOG

25. **Jumbles:** EMPTY RIVER TAMPER PLACED
    Answer: Regardless of where they traveled, this was the center of gravity—THE LETTER V

26. **Jumbles:** STAND GUMBO TWITCH OUTING
    Answer: The football coach was nervous about flying, so he was looking forward to this—TOUCHDOWN

27. **Jumbles:** PICKY VOCAL GENTLY BROKEN
    Answer: When their nuclear fusion experiment failed again, the scientists had—NO REACTION

28. **Jumbles:** FRONT BAGGY MINNOW PADDED
    Answer: Even with one, the thousand-dollar store was not going to be a success—GRAND OPENING

29. **Jumbles:** TACKY HABIT MUSSEL GAINED
    Answer: When the Pilgrims were presented with a feast, they did this—SAID THANKS

30. **Jumbles:** OCCUR COVET UNLOCK STRAND
    Answer: When there weren't enough go-carts to go around, they did this—TOOK TURNS

31. **Jumbles:** OFTEN GILLS EXOTIC DELUGE
    Answer: When the men entered the room for the speed dating, they went in—SINGLE FILE

32. **Jumbles:** EMPTY GULCH COOKIE PASTRY
    Answer: When the actor broke his leg on-stage, they had to—RECAST HIM

33. **Jumbles:** BLOOM WATCH STUFFY MIDDAY
    Answer: The groundhog made his prediction without a—SHADOW OF A DOUBT

34. **Jumbles:** GUARD LYING SURVEY ATTEND
    Answer: When no one showed up to buy her lemonade, she couldn't—STAND IT

35. **Jumbles:** MOVED SMELL OXYGEN ABACUS
    Answer: Once you've looked at one shopping center, you've—SEEN A MALL

36. **Jumbles:** BUDDY CRAMP BOUNTY STORMY
    Answer: When she asked if she would be able to get a seat on the next flight, she was told to—STAND BY

37. **Jumbles:** BLAZE HATCH OBJECT SAILOR
    Answer: Playing the sun in the play about the solar system allowed him to—BE A STAR

38. **Jumbles:** PRINT ALLOW CLASSY REVERT
    Answer: His unique sound system wasn't this—STEREOTYPICAL

39. **Jumbles:** CYCLE WOUND BEATEN BANTER
    Answer: The concert in Death Valley had—LOW ATTENDANCE

40. **Jumbles:** WAFER OZONE TALLER FACADE
    Answer: When the marathon runner missed the right turn, he ended up—LEFT ALONE

41. **Jumbles:** JUICE PLANK SLEEPY FIZZLE
    Answer: When her jigsaw puzzle was ruined, she did this—FELL TO PIECES

42. **Jumbles:** YEAST FABLE BOTHER EMBLEM
    Answer: His Valentine's Day lunch was this—A HEARTY MEAL

43. **Jumbles:** YUCKY PRIZE UNFAIR CATTLE
    Answer: Some people thought the Wright brothers were just—"PLANE" CRAZY

44. **Jumbles:** FAITH SCARF SCARCE WAFFLE
Answer: Careless drivers can end up—"CAR-LESS"

45. **Jumbles:** AWFUL STUNK DEFACE RESUME
Answer: Getting the flu on a Friday makes for this—
A "WEAK-END"

46. **Jumbles:** GRILL VENOM FLINCH BETRAY
Answer: In a leap year, which months have 29 days?—
ALL OF THEM

47. **Jumbles:** CONGA LARVA CRUNCH BESIDE
Answer: She was struggling in geometry class because there
was a—LEARNING CURVE

48. **Jumbles:** DRAFT ROUGH MASKED POETIC
Answer: Before their adventures at Yellowstone could begin,
they needed to do this—PARK THE CAR

49. **Jumbles:** UPPER ICING FORGOT ASTRAY
Answer: Putting the spire on the building was this—
TOP PRIORITY

50. **Jumbles:** KNELT SPURN ACTUAL TRENCH
Answer: The elephant needed a car with enough—
TRUNK SPACE

51. **Jumbles:** ALONG PSYCH UNRULY DINNER
Answer: He refused to draw the Jumble cartoon because the
idea behind it wasn't this—"PUNNY" ENOUGH

52. **Jumbles:** BLINK ADMIT SUFFIX GROCER
Answer: Elvis liked to eat meals that were this—
FIT FOR A KING

53. **Jumbles:** KNIFE DEPTH NEURON TRAUMA
Answer: When the unprepared hunter ran into the giant
buck, he said this—OH "DEER"

54. **Jumbles:** BRAWN FACET OUTFIT RODENT
Answer: After the success of his Model T, Henry expanded his
business because he could—AFFORD TO

55. **Jumbles:** ABIDE SPELL HOURLY TONGUE
Answer: When the birthing class instructor told a joke, he
got this—BELLY LAUGHS

56. **Jumbles:** HEDGE AVOID LETTER HORRID
Answer: When she needed to get to the hospital in a hurry,
she called a cab to DELIVER HER

57. **Jumbles:** SIXTH SLASH FUSION DRAFTY
Answer: When they announced the discovery of Pluto on
3-13-1930, people thought it was this—FAR OUT!

58. **Jumbles:** TEMPO GUEST HECKLE TANGLE
Answer: He did this to the other team when he made so
many baskets—SUNK THEM

59. **Jumbles:** SHOVE ODDLY UNWISE AROUND
Answer: The zombie was this when he warned that humans
were approaching—DEAD SERIOUS

60. **Jumbles:** AFOOT LAUGH RADIAL AFFORD
Answer: When James Watt talked about his steam engine,
some people thought he was—FULL OF HOT AIR

61. **Jumbles:** HUTCH ADAGE BEACON SORROW
Answer: After a long day of making cartoons, the Jumble
artist did this—DREW A BATH

62. **Jumbles:** DUNCE CHAMP SWITCH SQUASH
Answer: He was running behind with his mustard deliveries
and needed to do this—CATCH UP

63. **Jumbles:** UPEND DECAY ROOKIE FITTED
Answer: When he installed his new kitchen, he realized that
his granite was this—COUNTERFEIT

64. **Jumbles:** FLOOD SHOWN ENGINE ACCUSE
Answer: Breaking NHL records was this to Wayne Gretzky—
ONE OF HIS GOALS

65. **Jumbles:** GUESS CROWN FALLEN LIQUID
Answer: Their choice of Leonard Nimoy to play Spock was
this — LOGICAL

66. **Jumbles:** WEAVE DRUNK NOTION ISLAND
Answer: When they were up above Sydney, they were—
DOWN UNDER

67. **Jumbles:** SKIMP UNWED VORTEX INDIGO
Answer: When the waitress gave them the wrong cocktails,
they had—MIXED DRINKS

68. **Jumbles:** AWARE WHILE BEAUTY GATHER
Answer: Helen Hunt was anxious to star in "Twister" after the
script—BLEW HER AWAY

69. **Jumbles:** VIXEN GUILD SWATCH ABLAZE
Answer: The storm damaged the taxi when it did this—
HAILED A CAB

70. **Jumbles:** MADLY UNIFY UNPAID PEBBLE
Answer: How the pushy salesman said hello—"BUY-BUY"

71. **Jumbles:** ISSUE LOGIC INJURY AFFECT
Answer: When he asked the tailor to custom-make his
tuxedo, the tailor said—SUIT YOURSELF

72. **Jumbles:** BLEND IMPEL STATIC EASILY
Answer: People from Bangor who get carried away with their
state pride are—"MAINE-IACS"

73. **Jumbles:** ZESTY NIECE FAMOUS WRENCH
Answer: His attempt to impersonate Henry Winkler was
a—"FONZIE" SCHEME

74. **Jumbles:** MUSTY SIXTY NIBBLE FACTOR
Answer: When he put the finishing touches on his book
about clocks, his wife said this—IT'S ABOUT TIME

75. **Jumbles:** PLANT OUNCE SHOULD UPBEAT
Answer: How the math teacher expected her students to
respond—ON THE DOUBLE

76. **Jumbles:** GRUNT ELDER SHRINK APIECE
Answer: The ships left the port in a—CRUISE LINE

77. **Jumbles:** SOUPY FIGHT CAVITY GLITCH
Answer: After getting to the emergency room, he was
hoping for some—HOSPITALITY

78. **Jumbles:** MARRY ITCHY STUDIO SOCKET
Answer: When adding up how much rope he'd need for the
climb, he would do this — SUM IT

79. **Jumbles:** CRUSH THICK UNTOLD MEMORY
Answer: Regardless of the style it's performed in, a national
anthem is this—COUNTRY MUSIC

80. **Jumbles:** FAINT SKIMP OPAQUE MAYHEM
Answer: John McEnroe would sometimes lose his temper
trying to—MAKE HIS POINT

81. **Jumbles:** HAVOC EXCEL ADRIFT POCKET
Answer: Winning the pie-eating contest was this for him—
A PIECE OF CAKE

82. **Jumbles:** WINDY FAVOR RADIUS GIGGLE
Answer: They went to the zoo in Richmond to see a—
VIRGINIA WOLF

83. **Jumbles:** CRACK DIVOT ALWAYS GASKET
Answer: The concert by the volcano featured this—
LAVA ROCK

84. **Jumbles:** EXUDE ETHIC ZODIAC BUCKET
Answer: He went to Prague because he wanted to do this—
"CZECH" IT OUT

85. **Jumbles:** STUNG AGENT LOADED PURPLE
Answer: They went to the air show in Nebraska to see the—
GREAT "PLANES"

86. **Jumbles:** CRANK UNION DROOPY DEBTOR
Answer: The judge would be able to play tennis in his
backyard as a result of his—COURT ORDER

87. **Jumbles:** CHEER DRAWN FEMALE SUMMON
Answer: The gym at the military base strengthened the—
ARMED FORCES

88. **Jumbles:** AMAZE STYLE ABSORB CUDDLE
Answer: He wore goggles in the Mediterranean so he could
do this—"SEA" CLEARLY

89. **Jumbles:** AGONY MOURN ISLAND WICKED
Answer: The struggling actor became one when he got a part-time job as an usher—A LEADING MAN

90. **Jumbles:** USURP AWARD POTENT STINKY
Answer: He was this after finishing his first surfing lesson—WIPED OUT

91. **Jumbles:** MERGE AMUSE IDIOCY DECADE
Answer: When his sweet potato was undercooked, he did this—YAMMERED

92. **Jumbles:** ARENA DERBY MUSKET SMOOCH
Answer: The farmer called the vet to attend to the sick pig so that the pig could become a—CURED HAM

93. **Jumbles:** GAUGE POUND ASTRAY BOTANY
Answer: After examining the customer's ID, the waitress said, "Thank you for your—'PATRON-AGE'"

94. **Jumbles:** BLESS GUARD DOCKET CONVEX
Answer: The TV show about the fisherman has a—GOOD CAST

95. **Jumbles:** STRUM OFTEN DIFFER CAMERA
Answer: He became so good at putting up the sails that he did this—MASTERED IT

96. **Jumbles:** CABIN OMEGA ATTEND STRAND
Answer: After the guitarist donated his kidney, he became this—AN ORGANIST

97. **Jumbles:** BASIS HEFTY GOSSIP HYBRID
Answer: The church service atop the mountain received this—HIGH PRAISE

98. **Jumbles:** SILKY HYENA MUFFLE COLUMN
Answer: The winner of the hot dog eating contest was this—FULL OF HIMSELF

99. **Jumbles:** BRINK CREEK OCTANE BANTER
Answer: How the chiropractor saw his patients—BACK-TO-BACK

100. **Jumbles:** HUNCH MULCH LEVITY LOTION
Answer: She didn't like working on the new song with her bandmate, so she decided to—TUNE HIM OUT

101. **Jumbles:** BLANK GUMBO EATERY ACIDIC
Answer: The palace of Westminster is located near one in the Thames—A BIG BEND

102. **Jumbles:** GROOM THINK EFFORT MASCOT
Answer: After three bull's-eyes in a row, his goal of winning an Olympic gold medal was this—ON TARGET

103. **Jumbles:** SUSHI BEGAN SWIVEL INDICT
Answer: The conversation about current events while they fished resulted in—NEWS CASTS

104. **Jumbles:** MUSHY BOGUS DEFACE INFORM
Answer: He was this with his expensive fencing equipment—ON GUARD

105. **Jumbles:** SHYLY AWAKE SPLINT MARKET
Answer: What the diver didn't want to do—MAKE A SPLASH

106. **Jumbles:** FENCE DRINK WEASEL UNCORK
Answer: Winning the free art class was the—LUCK OF THE DRAW

107. **Jumbles:** AVIAN ADULT SPRUCE IRONIC
Answer: After a round of golf, the billionaire always left with his—DRIVER

108. **Jumbles:** HILLY MOVED DETECT WINERY
Answer: After his pine tree died, his neighbor did this—NEEDLED HIM

109. **Jumbles:** AGENT SCOFF DEFECT MONKEY
Answer: The attorney said this after her co-worker harassed her about her work—GET OFF MY CASE

110. **Jumbles:** INPUT RANCH TALLER ENOUGH
Answer: After bumping into some friends during his jog, he'd be this—RUNNING LATE

111. **Jumbles:** VOUCH LIGHT SMOKED OBLIGE
Answer: His speaker business was successful thanks to—HIGH VOLUME

112. **Jumbles:** EMPTY ABOVE TRENCH DECENT
Answer: Having an extra set of gloves in the glove compartment was—HANDY

113. **Jumbles:** AWARE FAITH DENTAL NUMBER
Answer: He opened his business here—NEW DELHI

114. **Jumbles:** EAGLE CRAMP STEREO POISON
Answer: The rock climber saw these when he went to buy new climbing equipment—STEEP PRICES

115. **Jumbles:** DAZED IVORY COPPER FAMOUS
Answer: His desire to own the biggest plumbing company in town was—A PIPE DREAM

116. **Jumbles:** CRUSH TIGHT HOBBLE WARMLY
Answer: After seeing that her dogs had dug up the back yard, she wanted the—"HOLE" TRUTH

117. **Jumbles:** WAFER SMELL DENOTE PELLET
Answer: Santa's helper was suffering from—LOW "ELF" ESTEEM

118. **Jumbles:** FACET EXCEL DIVERT BITTEN
Answer: What does December have that no other month has?—THE LETTER "D"

119. **Jumbles:** HIKER RODEO VOICED LOADED
Answer: The skunk hoodlums—"REEKED" HAVOC

120. **Jumbles:** IRONY BRING LESSON WINERY
Answer: His job at the mine was and wasn't—BORING

121. **Jumbles:** AGILE UNION RUDDER WAIVER
Answer: The Jumble artist's cartoon is a—LINE DRAWING

122. **Jumbles:** PIVOT CHURN MORTAL CASINO
Answer: The jury reached its decision with—CONVICTION

123. **Jumbles:** POUND SMIRK TRIPLE CASHEW
Answer: The model boats were ready to—SHIP IN TRUCKS

124. **Jumbles:** PRIMP GRILL PHOTON AFFIRM
Answer: When it came to which sandals she wanted to buy, the customer kept—FLIP-FLOPPING

125. **Jumbles:** SHIFT WOMEN PIRACY CELERY
Answer: The balloon was ascending perfectly, but the squabbling operators were going—NOWHERE FAST

126. **Jumbles:** SHYLY THANK PREFER CANCEL
Answer: The fish market's new slogan was a—CATCH PHRASE

127. **Jumbles:** PLUME ABATE SNEAKY SNITCH
Answer: The doctor would recover from his injuries if he could—BE PATIENT

128. **Jumbles:** WHARF MOUTH PLEDGE YONDER
Answer: Heidi Klum was working the minute she stepped off the plane because she was—A RUNWAY MODEL

129. **Jumbles:** RIVER WEDGE STRAND ROCKET
Answer: After seeing how much the bank's saving accounts earned, he was—INTERESTED

130. **Jumbles:** AROSE HOWDY YELLOW POETIC
Answer: Magellan set out to circumnavigate the globe and was able to—"SEA" THE WORLD

131. **Jumbles:** BASIS PRINT ABSURD SOCKET
Answer: When the guards at Alcatraz needed a rest, they took a—PRISON BREAK

132. **Jumbles:** TWEAK LEAVE DROOPY BUTTON
Answer: When she got new glasses, she—LOOKED BETTER

133. **Jumbles:** ADDED SPELL CANOPY BUTTER
Answer: The expectant mother tied everything to her—DUE DATE

134. **Jumbles:** CRUST FILMY COMMON JESTER
Answer: What she had when she saw her wedding cake—"TIERS" OF JOY

135. **Jumbles:** WIPER ONION BUSHEL AUBURN
Answer: The billionaire was able to enjoy the new yacht thanks to—OWNERSHIP

136. **Jumbles:** PENNY THINK LOCALE BUNKER
Answer: When the masseuse left her job, they wanted her to—KEEP IN TOUCH

137. **Jumbles:** BASIC APART PRIMER MUTINY
Answer: If politicians ever truly started to work together, then it would be—"BYE"-PARTISAN

138. **Jumbles:** CLASH COURT BROKER DIGEST
Answer: When she got sick after they set sail, he needed to get—BACK TO THE "DOC"

139. **Jumbles:** VENUE GLORY COUSIN ACTIVE
Answer: Running the cremation society made it possible for him to—"URN" A LIVING

140. **Jumbles:** GRAFT ADAGE DEFEAT HOOFED
Answer: After hiking down to the bottom of the Grand Canyon, they—GORGED

141. **Jumbles:** TRAWL ORBIT AGENCY PULPIT
Answer: He wasn't sure if he could give all his fortune to charity upon his death, but he was—WILLING TO TRY

142. **Jumbles:** OMEGA BROKE NAUSEA HERMIT
Answer: The horses in the barn were—"NEIGH-BORS"

143. **Jumbles:** VIXEN SWUNG FELONY MISHAP
Answer: All the recent construction was turning the street into—AN "AVE-NEW"

144. **Jumbles:** FENCE DRINK PARLOR MYSTIC
Answer: They needed one when they filmed the movie's bank robbery scene—A SECOND TAKE

145. **Jumbles:** RUMMY ENACT ELEVEN LOCKET
Answer: Love at first sight turned the butcher shop into a—"MEET" MARKET

146. **Jumbles:** THIEF STRUM GOVERN DAINTY
Answer: When the actors and actresses celebrated their Oscar award wins, it was a — STARRY NIGHT

147. **Jumbles:** QUILT CLOUT PROVEN DONKEY
Answer: If a penny came to life, it would become—"CENT-IENT"

148. **Jumbles:** BLOCK IVORY DEGREE SHOULD
Answer: The carpenter had a—GOOD BUILD

149. **Jumbles:** ABIDE TARDY PROFIT DEFECT
Answer: When he didn't have enough money to pay the taxi driver, he offered a—"FARE" TRADE

150. **Jumbles:** VALVE NACHO INSIST INDUCT
Answer: Her attempt to get away from Dracula was going to be—IN "VEIN"

151. **Jumbles:** STAND RATIO HOURLY DECENT
Answer: The strict ballet instructor kept his students—ON THEIR TOES

152. **Jumbles:** HAVOC PRONE DELUGE ZODIAC
Answer: After five marathon victories in a row, he lost... But he didn't mind...He'd—HAD A GOOD RUN

153. **Jumbles:** EAGLE MOUND NOTION PLACID
Answer: The zombie was such a good archer because his aim was—DEAD ON

154. **Jumbles:** GRAVE HUNCH THIRTY BABBLE
Answer: When they visited the capital of Germany in the frigid weather, they visited—"BURR-LIN"

155. **Jumbles:** APPLY EXPEL CHERRY MUFFLE
Answer: When she asked if she could use the spa coupon for a massage, they said—FEEL FREE

156. **Jumbles:** JUICY BLAZE PIMPLE VIRTUE
Answer: The pizza maker's award-winning slice won a—"PIECE" PRIZE

157. **Jumbles:** BISON TOTAL REVIVE FAMILY
Answer: She opened her flower shop when she was in her 70s because she was a—LATE BLOOMER

158. **Jumbles:** HIKER AGAIN NOODLE IMPACT
Answer: The movie about the winner of the marathon featured a—LEADING MAN

159. **Jumbles:** AFTER ORBIT SPLASH SMOGGY
Answer: The store owner's fake vomit and other disgusting novelties resulted in—GROSS PROFITS

160. **Jumbles:** TOOTH UTTER IMPALA APIECE
Answer: The captain of the plane was late for work after spending too much time as an—AUTO PILOT

161. **Jumbles:** UPROAR MINGLE WORTHY ISLAND SAFARI WALNUT
Answer: How Jeff Knurek kills time while waiting in line at the bank—WITH DRAWING

162. **Jumbles:** PRANCE HARDLY MOTION SHADOW SOCKET RAFFLE
Answer: The artists' stage performance was a—SKETCH COMEDY

163. **Jumbles:** TATTOO WARMTH FELLOW GENIUS IODINE ENGULF
Answer: The card shark attracted so much attention because he was a—FISH OUT OF WATER

164. **Jumbles:** HAPPEN BLURRY BISHOP PROVEN GLANCE AUTHOR
Answer: What the grandfather talked about when describing the good old days—"POP" CULTURE

165. **Jumbles:** JOGGER BETRAY FLAWED LEEWAY MINING STORMY
Answer: Gardening all day resulted in her—GROWING TIRED

166. **Jumbles:** FROSTY THROWN CLEVER ZENITH UNTOLD SLEEPY
Answer: Taking a left at the last intersection was a—TURN FOR THE WORSE

167. **Jumbles:** BAKING ARMORY SLUDGE OUTWIT CLERGY CAMERA
Answer: The dispute at the airport resulted in—BAGGAGE CLAIMS

168. **Jumbles:** REFUSE COLUMN AWHILE AIRING SUITOR SWAYED
Answer: There were able to win the hot-air balloon competition because they—GOT CARRIED AWAY

169. **Jumbles:** DOZING THATCH SPRAIN MIDDLE VIOLIN REGRET
Answer: Becoming the world's greatest soccer player was this—HIS LONG-TERM GOAL

170. **Jumbles:** ANYONE GUTTER BATTEN ASSURE SPOOKY ACIDIC
Answer: Magellan probably imagined himself circling the globe for years before he finally—GOT AROUND TO IT

171. **Jumbles:** SPRAWL UNPACK VOICED UPBEAT SOCKET FIASCO
Answer: The church with the plumbing problem was this—OUT OF SERVICE

172. **Jumbles:** AFFIRM GIBLET UNRULY SPRAWL SPOTTY HARDER
Answer: Producers didn't want Sylvester Stallone to star in "Rocky," so he—PUT UP A FIGHT

173. **Jumbles:** STITCH FIDDLE GROWTH AVENUE STRING STUDIO
Answer: The documentary about dictionary-maker Noah Webster was in—HIGH-DEFINITION

174. **Jumbles:** KNIGHT OUTLAW LAVISH ASTHMA TOMATO INDICT
Answer: His commute to work was this—TAKING A TOLL ON HIM

175. **Jumbles:** DREDGE OCCUPY FROZEN SOCIAL LAWFUL ENTICE
Answer: When he sat around the campfire with his buddies, he was with his—CIRCLE OF FRIENDS

176. **Jumbles:** TOWARD MUSSEL LATELY WRITER PROPER UTOPIA
Answer: When they put a wristwatch on the statue,—TIME STOOD STILL

177. **Jumbles:** AFRAID HUMBLE OUTING HEALTH FIERCE ODDITY
Answer: He was good at baseball—RIGHT OFF THE BAT

178. **Jumbles:** BALLAD LENGTH INSIST SPRAWL INFAMY TANDEM
Answer: When her sheep gave birth, Mary—HAD A LITTLE LAMB

179. **Jumbles:** DILUTE BEFORE HANGAR PUNDIT DOCTOR UTMOST
Answer: The NBA player didn't stand a chance with the WNBA player because she was this—OUT OF HIS LEAGUE

180. **Jumbles:** SCORCH LIZARD EITHER PANTRY GAZING BUSILY
Answer: He started bowling because he thought it would be this—RIGHT UP HIS ALLEY

Need More Jumbles®?

Jumble® Books

More than 175 puzzles each!

Cowboy Jumble®
ISBN: 978-1-62937-355-3

Jammin' Jumble®
ISBN: 1-57243-844-4

Java Jumble®
ISBN: 978-1-60078-415-6

Jazzy Jumble®
ISBN: 978-1-57243-962-7

Jet Set Jumble®
ISBN: 978-1-60078-353-1

Joyful Jumble®
ISBN: 978-1-60078-079-0

Juke Joint Jumble®
ISBN: 978-1-60078-295-4

Jumble® Anniversary
ISBN: 987-1-62937-734-6

Jumble® at Work
ISBN: 1-57243-147-4

Jumble® Ballet
ISBN: 978-1-62937-616-5

Jumble® Birthday
ISBN: 978-1-62937-652-3

Jumble® Celebration
ISBN: 978-1-60078-134-6

Jumble® Circus
ISBN: 978-1-60078-739-3

Jumble® Cuisine
ISBN: 978-1-62937-735-3

Jumble® Drag Race
ISBN: 978-1-62937-483-3

Jumble® Ever After
ISBN: 978-1-62937-785-8

Jumble® Explorer
ISBN: 978-1-60078-854-3

Jumble® Explosion
ISBN: 978-1-60078-078-3

Jumble® Fever
ISBN: 1-57243-593-3

Jumble® Fiesta
ISBN: 1-57243-626-3

Jumble® Fun
ISBN: 1-57243-379-5

Jumble® Galaxy
ISBN: 978-1-60078-583-2

Jumble® Garden
ISBN: 978-1-62937-653-0

Jumble® Genius
ISBN: 1-57243-896-7

Jumble® Geography
ISBN: 978-1-62937-615-8

Jumble® Getaway
ISBN: 978-1-60078-547-4

Jumble® Gold
ISBN: 978-1-62937-354-6

Jumble® Grab Bag
ISBN: 1-57243-273-X

Jumble® Gymnastics
ISBN: 978-1-62937-306-5

Jumble® Jackpot
ISBN: 1-57243-897-5

Jumble® Jailbreak
ISBN: 978-1-62937-002-6

Jumble® Jambalaya
ISBN: 978-1-60078-294-7

Jumble® Jamboree
ISBN: 1-57243-696-4

Jumble® Jitterbug
ISBN: 978-1-60078-584-9

Jumble® Journey
ISBN: 978-1-62937-549-6

Jumble® Jubilation
ISBN: 978-1-62937-784-1

Jumble® Jubilee
ISBN: 1-57243-231-4

Jumble® Juggernaut
ISBN: 978-1-60078-026-4

Jumble® Junction
ISBN: 1-57243-380-9

Jumble® Jungle
ISBN: 978-1-57243-961-0

Jumble® Kingdom
ISBN: 978-1-62937-079-8

Jumble® Knockout
ISBN: 978-1-62937-078-1

Jumble® Madness
ISBN: 1-892049-24-4

Jumble® Magic
ISBN: 978-1-60078-795-9

Jumble® Marathon
ISBN: 978-1-60078-944-1

Jumble® Neighbor
ISBN: 978-1-62937-845-9

Jumble® Parachute
ISBN: 978-1-62937-548-9

Jumble® Safari
ISBN: 978-1-60078-675-4

Jumble® See & Search
ISBN: 1-57243-549-6

Jumble® See & Search 2
ISBN: 1-57243-734-0

Jumble® Sensation
ISBN: 978-1-60078-548-1

Jumble® Surprise
ISBN: 1-57243-320-5

Jumble® Symphony
ISBN: 978-1-62937-131-3

Jumble® Theater
ISBN: 978-1-62937-484-03

Jumble® University
ISBN: 978-1-62937-001-9

Jumble® Unleashed
ISBN: 978-1-62937-844-2

Jumble® Vacation
ISBN: 978-1-60078-796-6

Jumble® Wedding
ISBN: 978-1-62937-307-2

Jumble® Workout
ISBN: 978-1-60078-943-4

Jumpin' Jumble®
ISBN: 978-1-60078-027-1

Lunar Jumble®
ISBN: 978-1-60078-853-6

Monster Jumble®
ISBN: 978-1-62937-213-6

Mystic Jumble®
ISBN: 978-1-62937-130-6

Outer Space Jumble®
ISBN: 978-1-60078-416-3

Rainy Day Jumble®
ISBN: 978-1-60078-352-4

Ready, Set, Jumble®
ISBN: 978-1-60078-133-0

Rock 'n' Roll Jumble®
ISBN: 978-1-60078-674-7

Royal Jumble®
ISBN: 978-1-60078-738-6

Sports Jumble®
ISBN: 1-57243-113-X

Summer Fun Jumble®
ISBN: 1-57243-114-8

Touchdown Jumble®
ISBN: 978-1-62937-212-9

Travel Jumble®
ISBN: 1-57243-198-9

TV Jumble®
ISBN: 1-57243-461-9

Oversize Jumble® Books

More than 500 puzzles each!

Generous Jumble®
ISBN: 1-57243-385-X

Giant Jumble®
ISBN: 1-57243-349-3

Gigantic Jumble®
ISBN: 1-57243-426-0

Jumbo Jumble®
ISBN: 1-57243-314-0

The Very Best of Jumble® BrainBusters
ISBN: 1-57243-845-2

Jumble® Crosswords™

More than 175 puzzles each!

More Jumble® Crosswords™
ISBN: 1-57243-386-8

Jumble® Crosswords™ Jackpot
ISBN: 1-57243-615-8

Jumble® Crosswords™ Jamboree
ISBN: 1-57243-787-1

Jumble® BrainBusters™

More than 175 puzzles each!

Jumble® BrainBusters™
ISBN: 1-892049-28-7

Jumble® BrainBusters™ II
ISBN: 1-57243-424-4

Jumble® BrainBusters™ III
ISBN: 1-57243-463-5

Jumble® BrainBusters™ IV
ISBN: 1-57243-489-9

Jumble® BrainBusters™ 5
ISBN: 1-57243-548-8

Jumble® BrainBusters™ Bonanza
ISBN: 1-57243-616-6

Boggle™ BrainBusters™
ISBN: 1-57243-592-5

Boggle™ BrainBusters™ 2
ISBN: 1-57243-788-X

Jumble® BrainBusters™ Junior
ISBN: 1-892049-29-5

Jumble® BrainBusters™ Junior II
ISBN: 1-57243-425-2

Fun in the Sun with Jumble® BrainBusters™
ISBN: 1-57243-733-2